I0790605

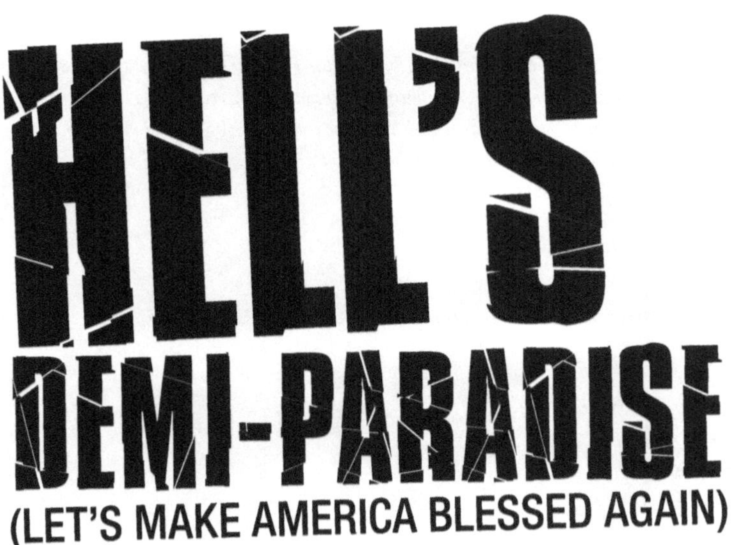

HELL'S DEMI-PARADISE

(LET'S MAKE AMERICA BLESSED AGAIN)

Sequel to *Miracles and Madness*

JACK HALL

iUniverse®

**HELL'S DEMI-PARADISE (LET'S MAKE AMERICA BLESSED AGAIN)
SEQUEL TO MIRACLES AND MADNESS**

iUniverse books may be ordered through booksellers or by contacting:

iUniverse
1663 Liberty Drive
Bloomington, IN 47403
www.iuniverse.com
844-349-9409

Because of the dynamic nature of the Internet, any web addresses or links contained in this book may have changed since publication and may no longer be valid. The views expressed in this work are solely those of the author and do not necessarily reflect the views of the publisher, and the publisher hereby disclaims any responsibility for them.

Any people depicted in stock imagery provided by Getty Images are models, and such images are being used for illustrative purposes only.
Certain stock imagery © Getty Images.

ISBN: 978-1-6632-0621-3 (sc)
ISBN: 978-1-6632-0622-0 (e)

Print information available on the last page.

iUniverse rev. date: 08/05/2020

CONTENTS

PREFACE

THE CORE OF PESTILENCE

Unless we return to the ancestral garden where the luscious "apple" and the illustrious woman faced off over the word, the law and the absolute, know that death awaits in the gloom.

As America and the world suffers its most deadly pandemic all we know is where it originated and its possible link to a military lab where diseased bats were being weaponized for unspecified cause. Never since President Nixon awakened the sleeping giant has this prodigal son sought to overtake its handmaiden in economic and military predominance. While the Marxist United Front originates to destroy capitalism and fifty years hence while our precious resource was advancing freedom abroad, the nation internal had been subverted into hells immoral cesspool.

With the face of God turned and the culture totally and institutionally compromised by an alien godless indoctrination, all hope must revert to what has never been taught of a retributive justice. A half century since God has been rendered obsolete in his own freedom inspired Christian enlightened Eden II paradise the culture is on life support. A subversive socialist illiterate loon ravishes our cities, topples our monuments and loots established businesses while the demon-crat mayors and governors in bed with socialist demands remain mute. Nowhere during this double edge sword of an economic and social pandemic are there stirrings of a revived Sons of Liberty counter revolution. Nor is there a call of retribution towards our taxpayer funded university hotbeds of sedition that fuels the violence. And as the nation is in stage two of potential lockdown in the face of bankruptcy over trillions spent on guaranteed non work income, let's turn our attention to the hypotheticals that lost America "the right of passage".

First, we must return to the apple and the ancestral garden. Neither banishment nor the curse was because of the apple perse but of the miracle seed that represents the total plan of creation. The luscious apple and its tree of good and evil was Gods symbol that heaven and earth were dual entities cast in a positive and negative unity. Every atom building block except hydrogen the first, lightest and most abundant will contain a matter proton a stabilizing neutral neutron stem and the generative electron. God was on hand to praise all that was good of electron essence. Opposing God was the viper antagonist representing the amoral objective proton. On one side the spirit of good and righteous conduct and in opposition all that was foreboding in evil.

Unfortunately, script at the creation was the American divinely inspired fortress that would nurture the great Christian moralizer of Godly essence. Now in barely two centuries we've sided with the viper in turning God's most proud nation into a scorched earth hells demi-paradise.

The envenemous tongue that survived the great flood and were the executioners of Christ have lived on to subvert and subjugate America by a barbarous anti-God Marxist neo-science. Our demise by fiery false opposition has its direct tracing to the ancestral apple with one caveat. The new apple has bisect the seed of creation by exhibiting only hells prototype that totally abolishes the electron generative truth.

Encased in its own handheld small screen universe and touch pad brain it can in Nano-seconds direct its unbalanced imbecilic hoards into any city, town or memorial as a plaque of destruction. As many pray for God to send his army of angel to purge the demon-crat socialist onslaught we must ask, what remains of the precious fruit of the tree that is worth saving? What has not been bartered away by a villainous Marxist united front and a sleeping giant prodigal son we awakened? Who stole our Godly inheritance and ponders the next move to steal our identity?

My guess is of a Trump card called the mighty laser whose stolen technology is at work directing the onslaught of destructive storms, and what an uncanny way to transport a lethal pandemic aboard the trade wind messenger of life. Ask yourself why our trade wind states of Florida, Texas, California, Arizona and others watch covid case continue to rise unabated? Has anyone questioned why the confiscation of S. Sea islands or puppet state influence in Venezuela, Cuba, Panama and others located between the equator and 15 degrees north? In this sensitive zone diurnal heat is rising by convection that is cooled and falls as rain before directed by Coriolis force onshore. Never mind that scoundrels now play God with this miracle transparent asset.

THE TRUTH FAILED TO TEACH

Plus and minus, positive and negative in-capsuled in every atom building block of a seed existence never crossed the threshold of education. Both are opposites in contradiction and conflict and unless they are unified in oneness there is chaos.

For this reason when God's word of positive and negative one was script to the atom, all 106 will have a neutron balancing stem except hydrogen the first, the lightest and most numerous. Both were on a one to one basis immune from conflict. In nature they remain unified meaning everything positive charge must aspire to the moral custody of the electron. Unity connotes deference to the most moral opposite. Unless man understood and taught this masterful truth of duality the law of contradictory opposites would fall prey the scavengers of truth we know as anarchists, Marxists, socialists and liberal secularists. The reason negative force was barred from education was because to do so meant the need to teach of sin.

INTRODUCTION

Just as my trusting pen retired from its battle to save America, Hell's Pandora's Box opened threatening the extinction of humanity. Not unlike the phantom Black Death plaque of the 14th Century claimed to begin in China, this contagion also came without warning or a victim's hint of protection.

Between its time of breakout in December or January it was not until the ides of March that its mysterium of death reached America. Once the name Wuhan surfaced the world was led to believe that the pestilence arose from an outdoor market where live animals including bats were sold. No mention that a short distance away was a bio lab where experimental offensive weapons existed, using animal diseases to be super bombarded and weaponized as the ultimate instrument of death for neutralizing a potential enemy. We can only speculate knowing that neither the World Health Organization nor American assistance was welcomed as with journalistic coverage to ameliorate the problem.

The American press accepted the specious fabrication to favor the Demon-crats who welcomed any ploy to unseat President Trump. For certain never were relations more strained between East and West since the Nixon administration awakened the sleeping giant. When this happened according to Toynbee it would make the world tremble. Not until Donald Trump became president was there determined effort to thwart the Chinese piranha from sucking the country dry in unbalanced trade, jobs, industry and the damnable theft of American inventive genius.

The American scattering of its economic and military base prior to the Trump crackdown on tariffs, money manipulation and theft was not unlike when the Jewish people were scattered throughout the world. After all, if they could confiscate and weaponize islands in international waters, why not animal diseases, or to blame America as the conspirator rattus-ratus whose military planted the lethal pestilence.

To ask of this apocalyptic occurrence that has brought imminent death and disease, a government need to shut down its industrial base, loss of a work force, depletion of food and sundry supplies, a lockdown of travel and mandatory social distancing fraught with fear, anxiety and concern for what is to follow. The answer lies both in our dust laden sacred instruction guide as well as quotes from an appended Shakespeare, "the fault dear Brutus is not in our stars but in <u>ourselves</u> that we have grown so great as to have lost the breed of noble bloods.

I need not remind you who among us are the sinister "noble blood" who would honor the eternal devil and his one world order of tyrannical socialist dominance rather than follow the divine promises of our founding in a Trump presidency.

That brings us to our modern day appended Chinese enemy made lucid by the eternal devils reworking of the <u>Prodigal Son</u> parable of Jesus. Never fail to consider that in this world of opposites the satanic fallen angel was more adept of the ways of God than we mortals. As the sleeping giant was welcomed with open arms in hopes it would become humble and beholden to its western stewardship the strategy proved futile. If anything, the aid and assistance only emboldened the communist brigand to secretly and unlawfully plot the American demise.

When this pandemic passes without a forsaken follow-up "trap" this may be freedoms wake-up call to follow Washington's departing advice to end all economic entangling alliances with both the invisible and the real devil. Demand that our industry returns home and if it can't be produced here let us turn to our neglected Central and South American Christian brotherhood who would never forsake us. Then let us bind up our wounds by bringing prayer and bible reading back. Next we must unite to stop the sacrificing of our beloved infants to the demon Moloch. Lastly, we must purge and purify our national capital now dishonored of its mission to administer the justice of a freedom inspired Christian enlightened natural law.

BACK TO OUR PAGAN ROOTS

Time has passed for anyone to ask if this pandemic was God's will. All twenty three preceding cultures surely questioned what force or external power fostered their demise. Had we followed our creator's natural moral law as bound in our coveted Constitution and not replaced it with man's civil law of the jungle, the answer was succinct. All things of a seed creation reach their natural conclusion of birth, atrophy and death. Any mitigating circumstance rest between the nature of the cell and the generative life force of animated principle. Not by serendipitous chance or fortuitous choice but by a deprecating ignorance has America by forgery of freedom abandoned inspired moral truth to author the fear of death of a nefarious hell.

A demon-crat self-righteous belief that freedom was man made crucified every remaining word of the cross to make America the most carnal and savage nation on Earth. Never to pay heed that America was an honored relic of the cross to accompany freedom as its moral agent, allowed a hedonist transformation that has atrophied the world's greatest social miracle to become as hay, chaff and stubble.

Even a fallen angel of Godly potential was well aware that when time stood between the barbarian and civilization, time was on the side of the demonic one. So beware the ides of March that like the thief in the night turned light into darkness, heaven into hell and freedom as the generative essence of God from hope into fear, anxiety into isolation and the viral soul to languish in hell.

For those who survive the pestilence whether now or later allegiance must be made either to our founding God inspired principles or with the required mark of the evil one whose end result in order to buy or sell was now in jeopardy by a manufactured viral attachment to paper coin and plastic currency. This plaque has welcomed demand for the implanted chip and triple six marking on the forehead and hand. No longer were we exemplars of the alpha and omega whose pinions were our defense against evil reproach.

HELLS-DEMI-PARDISE

Demi means half as in Demi-god. And because our secondary universe was conceived as half objective matter annealed in a fiery state of hell, then made whole by a subjective Godly "Essence", required we junior gods unify the extremes or suffer the inequities. From the creators plan we were given a "free will" backed by a retributive justice of reward or punishment for this endeavor.

Unfortunately a gentile pagan ancestry preferred to bisect heaven from hell and look to natures material desires as the paradigm for excellence. They saw Gad and nature as one which made idol worship popular. Little did they realize that nature like man was the handiwork of God. America likewise would devolve from traditional belief unwilling to accept freedoms moral standards. Motivated by a scientific realism God has now been neutered by a liberal and progressive mindset of a false utopia. After two centuries the verdict is in as the nation writhes in horror.

The last time this glorified nation was faced with the plaque of difference and division an admired "rail-splitter" with malice toward none and charity for all pioneered a new unity. This new plaque we face is a virulent political sepsis out to choke our founding principles in exchange for a spiteful neo-pagan Obama-nation transformational socialist hell on earth. These modern assassins are not of the rail-splitting working class founded on a faith driven ethic, but a "God is dead" hundred year communist ploy to destroy a Judeau-Christian capitalist inspired paradise.

Facing the new peril by divine providence is a "businessman railer" with love of country and staunch belief to liberate a subversive liberal bondage. His adversary is a demon-crat, neo pagan, neo barbarian scurvy whose animas is against God, country, Christianity, capitalism, the founding fathers, our Jewish appendage, national borders, a strong military, a border wall, voting standards, termination of infanticide, low taxation, gun ownership, immigration control, border patrol, the police, biologic sexual identity, CO2 emissions, the Electoral College, prayer and bible reading in schools, disparity of income, natural law and the flag. They oppose conservative principles that placed God as the sovereign over weather and climate and the DNA code that makes each of us a child of God.

To lose a national election is an act of war to their erratic conscience. Children have become their pawn of fear to ballyhoo fossil fuel as the cause for catastrophe. Never would they consider that carbon deposits both positive and negative charged were widely dispersed by the creator above and below ground to facilitate a generative electron energy source for the duration of human existence. With it came purifying censors no fact of man could ever comprehend.

Listen up little ones and take notice to the miracle clouds that of power and glory silently transport an ocean little by little in purity to nourish the seeds of living form. Rejoice to their four eternal pillars of earth, air, fire and water that fluctuate as one in their climatic act of love. Also, when the faithful evangels brought Christianity from the cross to the American repository, safe from His son's despotic pagan crucifixion, the bountiful industrial revolution was freedoms redemptive ransom for its deliverance.

I also believe that a revival of American greatness in in preparation to assist our Israeli appendage in the fast approaching tribulation pre-curser to Armageddon. Be ever mindful that the same electron essence of freedoms God lives within every cell of being that communicates as one to educate, nourish and heal every malady in need of soullear unity. The secret is to summon the magical power through His merciful stripes and broken body in defense of our sins.

THE WORD OF ONE

In a dual creation of a heaven and hell unity, of necessity, there had to be from the finite to the infinite a dual language and mathematics. One, imperfect of object conceived in fire and another pure and eternal in divine essence. Make no mistake America was not conceived by hells imperfect and corruptible, but by a cynosure spirit absolute for a divine necessity. Providential trust was for the security of Christ's admonitions should Israel default on the imperative of His kingdom on earth.

In retrospect the free will inevitability would lead to the crucifixion followed by the destruction of Rome and a thousand year return to the soil for a decentralized restructuring of the human soul. In this simple justice setting life's focus was on the afterlife in unity with a material dowry wrought by exploration, discovery and settlement before the long trek to the American fortress. Close behind was an industrial age made manifest by freedoms love.

Although the scribes will pen the 15th century Renaissance as a rebirth in learning it was in truth the Christian Evangels coming face to face with their opposing weeds of hell, staking out a claim by an atheistic science to choke their righteous cause.

Just as death is our companion at conception so also will every good and blessed aspect of life be confronted with the opposite. I'm not convinced that the dueling of opposites was a manifestation of Eden but a necessary means for purifying the good, the true and the beautiful from the proponents of hell. I made this assumption from the introductory line of the world's greatest instructive scriptural guide ever written. In that opening statement lays the answer to every question regarding the conflicts arising from a heaven and hell unity. Pay heed to the following statement. "In the beginning was the word and the word was one in God."

Make note that when the atheistic antagonists of Christianity finally get a socialist name recognition they will abolish a beginning and institute the fake hypothesis that creation evolved by happenstance absent a plan or a planner. And today its liberal followers are ensconced ready for takeover. So the following secret to survival may well become the prologue for demise.

Like unto the Golden Rule, etched on our mind forever, was the proverbial definition of the word "one", chances are that it is the only single most remembered definition for trusted recall as follows: "One refers to person, place, or thing that has weight and occupies space." Nothing was ever more succinct of half-truth and all lie.

So what about the invisible and invincible of "one," that is not of object but of subject and is absolute in the ideal quality of person, place and thing as a spiritual essence? Its name is absolute one and is responsible for the generation of a total atom seed creation of ubiquitous variety. How do we know this? We know this from the above introduction of our survival guide. The absolute word of one is a vertical axis that is inscribed inside the ellipse as the physical form for all created object be it of human head of body or of all earthly bodies.

Only once in my eighty nine years having lived through all or part of fifteen presidents, a Great Depression, followed by a World War and fifty years dealing with education, did I hear vague mention of absolute "one". It happened in the elementary grade of a mountain top school in Central Pennsylvania, center of the universe to me.

That rare morning a teacher inadvertently made mention that "one" was the only number that on one side carried the plus sign and the other the minus. The affect had the response of an air raid announcement to duck and take cover as was common in those days. But this time all sat stationary with hands raised to question the anomaly. Immediately the teacher replied 'they cancel one another out.' For most the answer sufficed but for me as I look back, mine was the prefrontal cortex to pursue the Holy Grail cup sought after since the Last Supper. Was I so positioned for a mysterious mission as many are so graced to pursue?

If that was my pre-ordained goal then the same invincible that prefaced our scriptural instruction manual with the words, "in the beginning was the word and the word was "one" in God, was my pathfinder as well.

Even after a half century lag time of an avocation in education never again did I hear scholarly reference to a plus and minus one. But regardless like the all-powerful adamant stone this spiritual titan became a prisoner of my mind, something of its latent truth was forever pleading to be set free. Akin to the secret DNA code for cellular growth and potential this invisible luminary was shadow mastering a freedom entitled Holy Spirit companion to comfort my every need so it seemed.

Finally, the Eureka moment arrived but not in the same fashion as when Archimedes discovered the specific gravity for gold while attending the Roman baths. His moment of discovering sent him running naked into the street shouting: Eureka! I found it. With the world a much different place now than Ancient Greece, my discovery of absolute plus and minus one would have met the same fate as the most entrancing DNA sculpture did.

What should have been the worlds most honored discovery would fizzle when one of its scientific discoverers named Watson, before he died, was asked how he thought the DNA was implanted in the human gene replied; "Possibly by aliens." This doomed its miracle as just another matter particle. It would join the electron generative essence of God on the scrap heap of matters inert slag alongside God's natural law, unity and His absolute word of one.

My revelatory find that led to the greatest truth behind every creation mystery of this dual miracle of diametric extremes once again stirred my soul like the maturing infant in the mother's womb, this time as both a Eureka moment and one of pity as well. For this we must look to Albert Einstein, possibly the greatest analytical agnostic scientist since Newtown. Now in his waning years as professor emeritus at Princeton University he was working on a problem that baffled him most of his life. It was called the unified field theory which involved the two fundamental forces of a heaven and earth universe, those of gravitation and electromagnetism. If he could unite the positive force of gravity and the negative of energy into one positive charged matter equation then heaven and its sovereign God could be forever eviscerated and matters Big Bang the acclaimed god of creation. When I read that Einstein had failed in his matter theory the Eureka moment exploded in by brain and absolute one as the word of God was freed but only in vain.

How sad that Einstein's failure to unify inert matter and God's electron wave into one unifield matter theory failed to turn an atheistic science on its head. This was the catalyst for science to immediately form unity with God as an act of penitence for a mortal defiance of truth. Rather it only emboldened them when two years after Einstein's death the Russians launched "Sputnik" the first earth orbiting satellite that put science at the helm of entering the race into space. Five years hence prayer and bible reading will exit the American school and public forum clearing the way for the mass murder of the embryonic miracle of life.

By shrewd frame of deception the word infant in the sacred womb will be changed to fetus, as if it was worthless chattel. This paved the way for its sterilization and solution to control an overpopulation Malthusian hoax to join that of global warming.

This better explains why God sent only one apostle that of Paul or Saul of Tarsus to minister the gentile pagan unbeliever. We must praise God incessantly in prayer for the converts who forged the greatest experiment of an unwritten faith driven freedom inspired body and soul American contribution of His pure and holy love.

While America has failed, God is again sifting the unbelievers throughout the world in advance of a world conversion. In this world of opposites what fact of science can explain why, when the virtuous good seed is planted in sprouts being accompanied by its unproductive weed that human hands did not plant. Or why at the moment of conception each of us are accompanied by an avenger called death. This dichotomy of opposites was not a decision of "Big Bang". I do believe however that it was an absentee landlord's way of secretly judging the will to unify and take dominance of the destructive weed or make compromise and fall prey to its evil stranglehold.

Be cautious of the historian scribe who personifies the 15th century Renaissance as a rebirth of science and learning after the fall of Rome. Never is it mentioned as the first face to face meeting of hells deathly ministers and heavens resurrected angels of light about to strategize which will be victorious. In real terms it was the evangels on their long trek to the American sanctuary and the opposing athiestic upstarts of their glorified weed of science in names like Marx, Freud, Darwin, Nietzsche and others fearing what effect the crucifixion had on the demise of Rome, were eager to recapture its bygone romanticism. It was there where two roads converged from the beautiful Robert Frost "the road not taken." One was reserved for the self-enfranchised socialist secular brigand who would veer right preaching equality of the masses by civil law takeover of the laws of capitalist production and distribution of wealth. While you and I were in company with the evangels who veered left with their azimuths aligned to the guiding star of the east in pursuit of freedoms new home that gleefully awaits.

It was not by chance that the despotic realists gained converts from the working class before being exiled out of Germany on their way to Russia. Here they would stage a brutal revolution, kill the Czars and begin a campaign to expropriate the land of the peasants under penalty of death and forced labor gulags for political opponents. Not to belabor the effects of this godless capitalist hating system only to caution what could be a repeat performance if America falls prey to the Marxist campaign rhetoric that is now preaching equality of every obscure cause whether of health, finance, class or concern.

What began as an Obama transformation sent the national debt from nine to twenty trillion and if this Bolshevists brigand is ever elected learn what the word expropriates means. It means to take possession of ones ownership for the public good in land, production and distribution.

I am hopeful the president Trump savior will prevent this from ever happening as it appears his mission is foreordained. None the less, it behooves us to revisit the honored motto of, "know thyself" in the age starved for love and our schools preaching the Marxist liberalism of civil law equality when by natural law nothing in creation is equal but death and opportunity. Equality of difference is responsible for beauty and a coded excellence by inequality of difference. God was well aware that equality of difference would put the corruptible of matter or the same plain or above the virtuous and pure which for many is the case. Equality of difference destroys the knowledge of self as the arbiter of every man's fortune, which the socialist liberal hucksters advocate to get elected. Their remedy for self is worse than any disease.

Unfortunately in an age where God has been dethroned and the mother as God's surrogate to charge the infants soul is now replaced by the inanimate amoral puppeteers. Starved for love the wizards of objective smart rushed in to fill a void which was more an open pit covered with thatch used in Vietnam to catch a menacing tiger. None the less the wizards of fact hit on their mother lode of fool's gold and harnessed it to an illumined hand held material universe. Copied from the spiders web famous for capturing its prey was now improvised by hijack of the electron wave to sensitize the universal mind for reclaim of its neo-pagan material self. We know this touch screen of a fool's purgatory was a façade to placate a prestige of Facebook or twitter dignity but of what effect on the inner self temperance, self-control or piety of will.

Finally, in a world where what goes around comes around, is it degrading of sense to ask the following. Did the seductive apple of Eve's eye have any correlation to the deceptive magic of today's material seductive giant called Apple?

THE ANOMALY OF IGNORANCE

With all things a cause and a purpose, a plan and a planner, America was a "late comer" to the world of nations for a little known cause. Before pure freedom as creations most powerful force could be made a human attribute it had to await an Israeli freewill rejection of his Son's Christian admonitions. Once the pagan crucifixion occurs, freedoms anointing and moralizing spirit of worship must be redirect to nestle in the pre-ordained American plantation, safe and secure from despotic tyrants and authoritarian enemies. Another little perceived sad reality is that God will dispatch only one apostle, Paul or Saul of Tarsus, to minister to the pagan gentile converted believer, for that long and arduous anointed trek.

Need we opine of the Creator's fore knowledge of sending eleven apostles to the Jew knowing that Christian brotherhood was no match for a gentile pagan betrayerhood. Surely that is why America would transcend from the most morally blessed on earth to exhibit the most evil of its coveted constitutional guarantees.

Ancestry.com is famous for taking one back to a branch of the tree but never to the clan or tribe of its heavenly root. Please forgive my inquisition of the gentile American idol worshipping pagan genesis as belonging to the tribe of Levi. From our instruction guide they were rebuked by God as wicked stubble, losing all shares of inheritance.

For those who grew in the faith and kept His holy conservative precepts and their love of Israel, the need is to implore entreaty with the apostle and bring anew America as the honored repository for Christian souls.

Also to caution how our Jewish appendage underwent numerous scattering and suffering both abroad and by invading forces that left the land desolate for centuries. In fact Mark Twain will log of it barren, uninhabitable condition on one of his world travels in the nineteenth century. We should juxtapose this to Israel's modern day glorious reparation of the productive land and return of its people in preparation, I believe, for the tribulation period and second coming.

Unbeknownst to most gentile, America will have its own scattering, not of people but of industry, jobs, trade, intellectual property and most important a political polarization between liberal sense and Gods rejuvenating force of essence. Few gentiles see this dichotomy of difference as providence preparing the meridians in advance of the competing ideological forces of good and evil. Again Israel will be centerfold in what is destined by revelation to right a world that has lost its way.

Instead of a damnable and idiotic transformation of the greatest political and economic system of the world there should be a unifying effort to purge the land of a liberal Marxist progressive enemy of pure freedom. All quadrants of liberal and conservative should lock conflicting genomes to restore a renewed faith in freedoms much maligned God. Let us have as a backdrop the honored dead and wounded who in the past half century gave their last full measure of devotion while at home a united front liberal subversion desecrated this hallowed ground our brave patriots fought to keep free.

Following are imperatives worth pursuing to heal the scars of a neo-pagan, neo-barbarism, demon-crat anomaly of ignorance. The most important attributes the God of freedom gave us to combat ignorance beside the faith of conscience was the sacred ballot. Instead of focusing on the Russian menace which in theory has for a hundred years subvert, demonized, and dumbnified every virtuous act of institutional and human judgement, let us turn this age of foolishness into an age of wisdom. Immediately realize that next to death as a universal pre-existing condition the need is to recognize the moral infection that is at the root of the physical.

In this season of darkness we can still enjoy both worlds but only by resurrecting the crucified word of our covenantal God. This may be our last chance to purge the demon-crat liberal socialist bandoleers vying to transform freedom into an authoritarian tyranny.

As masters of illusion by defrocking pure freedom as the essence of God gave them civil law control over the freedom to regulate climate, fossil fuel, carbon burning engines, CO2 emission s and the termination of living embryo. By distrust for a spiritual humanity allowed their justification of an objective freedom to follow the Freudian concept of infantile neuroticism by mandating a schools nurse's office to dispense of birth control pills, condoms and abortion counselling. Some of their more progressive advocates even raised concern over animal flatulence as a global concern. Ever wonder what our inspired founding fathers would say of their "Big Bang" immoral lawless replacement? Surely their hatred for the principles of truth and tradition was grounds to oust an evil party and replace it with one of unity aligned to natural law.

THE LAW

Evil spelled backwards is live and natural law turned inside out becomes the civil law bane of live in evil. Anyone who perceives of the miraculous whole of this illusive rhythmical creation and not sense of a high moral law that no fact can explain is devoid of reason. Not only is it the fountain stone of creation and maxim of truth but thankfully, the anchor pin for the world's greatest freedom inspired Christian enlightened Eden II envy of the world.

From its inspired word and eternal percepts our providential founders mold the laws of our constitution in defense of eternal laws governing life, liberty, property, opportunity, speech, religion, the right to bear arms in defense of autocratic tyrants in the pursuit of happiness. It was the mastermind for a trifecta separation of powers republic with enumerated powers for the federal and reserved left to the states granting a check and balance with the Supreme Court as formal arbitrator of disputes.

God knew that freedom alone does not make a nation virtuous. For this reason man as a being of divine love needed more than nature itself to bring him into unity with the eternal principles of the soul. For this reason alone, Christ was sent to inscribe the law of divine natural principle for living perfection on the hearts of men. It should have been an established truth that before America was conceived as the earthly model of authentic freedom that Christian law must become its moralizing helpmate companion.

Christianity, which has now gone from the ivory tower of light to the darkened recesses of the gutter, needs to be reclaimed not as a religion but as the metaphysical law to purge and purify what remains of freedom. The word of God was not meant as a religion but as an eternal truth. Every American whether saint or sinner has just witnessed over three years of

Gethsemane as we sat spellbound with our cup of hemlock. Simply stated, now that natural law embodied in the world's greatest constitution, its declaration and maxim of the divine soul, has been eviscerated by the demon-crat liberal assassins, and the outcome of their unjust impeachment over, by the will of God let them drink the hemlock.

To not recognize the difference between the subjecting natural law and its opposing of man's objective improvised "civil" law of the jungle was a defect of education, although it had nothing to do with religion and more about a liberal denunciation of paying homage to the cynosure of an eternal mind spirit.

By evading the knowledge of a dual heaven and earth unity no child would ever recognize the meaning of mind over matter or matter over mind reality. This would abrogate the teaching of good vs. evil or freedom vs. tyranny as it relates to sin. No child will learn the natural law truth that pure freedom of which perpetual motion and mathematical perfections exhibit its truth, was created never to make compromise with the restraints of evil. Yet they are taught the liberal objective opposite to release these pent-up Freudian inhibitions and frolic with the debilitating aftereffects that should alarm us all. Against our founders inspired will the truths that made us a God reliant people have been negated and made subject to the imprecations of evils affliction.

Never educated on the merits of natural law, the civil law of the jungle has brought to the fore the left leaning liberal piranha now ensconced in the nation's capital. As they seem to devour every virtuous asset of natural law with a hate filled rubric laced with the Marxist united front lie, nearly half of our cut flower generation pay homage with the word yes!

And who is to blame for their indoctrinated attraction to an old Bolshevik presidential contender? Civil law is an amoral contract with the devil although not openly espoused by the governor of the big apple. He recently stated that; "civil law" takes precedence over natural law. This is the law the godless liberal faction refers to when they accuse a president of any and everything of the vaunted lie.

Now that the neo-pagan pantheists have bisect us from our Christian roots tyranny is on the rise and immortality all around us. We've reached the new normal where the good of innocence has no defense and the basis for law is without moral consequence. How often under these conditions have we heard the voice from the estranged left proselytize the slogan; "no one is above the law." Yet never are they asked by which law are they referencing. Certainly the law which the liberal activists promulgate is not the natural law of our freedom inspired founders sacred constitution.

The demon-crat transforming lunatic now ensconced in the nation's capital proselytizing the civil law of revised Marxist lies and innuendo to impeach the president was more frightening than words can describe. As we begin to ask ourselves how to disband this grotesque gargoyle squad of weird attire and painted lip their stranglehold on sacred tradition prompts a farmer's query. After finding a turtle perched atop a fence post his three questions should concern us all. Where did the turtle come from, how did it get there and of what good is it now that it's here?

These questions we must ask in defense of our sacred traditions as to how a nation's house of the peoples will, could be under siege. As we ponder how they got here, who vetted them at the ballot box and of what good do they serve the nation? Especially, while at the same time their Bolshevik replacements are out sewing the evil seeds that if elected will destroy the greatest freedom inspired, Christianed enlightened Eden II paradise on earth.

I was there in 1962 when an atheist in a nearby school district sued by "civil law" to have prayer and bible reading removed from education. A liberal "civil law" Supreme Court will usurp that respected right of natural law and concur by passing a nationwide ban on school prayer. Five years prior to the ban the Russians would shock the world by launching "Sputnik", the first ever earth orbiting satellite. Imagine awakening that morning knowing that every hour we were being surveilled by a pretentious indefensible enemy. Almost immediately an atheistic science will become the quasi "catchup" headmaster of education. More than a "wake-up call" for an overhaul of math and science another life changing tragedy had stepped up to fill the vacuum left when the power of God's word was extricated.

At first the principal tried filling the mental void by reading samples of poetic verse. Not only did the idea boomerang but so did its replacement of several minutes of reflective silence. Within days our first drug victim arrived having overdosed on a horse tranquilizer. Then came the news that one of our junior high students had succumbed after being made to drink battery acid. With dress and deportment taking its toll an administrative decision called for the harebrained need to restructure all curriculums around self-esteem. Although the idea came from the left coast where the problem began it was quite odd to see musical chairs become the centerpiece of some classes. For the first time there were full time guidance counselors for every grade aided by a school psychiatrist and psychologist. A matter oriented objective non-moral solution was proof that neo-paganism and its barbaric advocate had arrived.

With science in the driver's seat and Big Bang the honorary replacement to God's vacated throne, most ill-educated civil law neo-pagans had little concern that separate but equal was a liberal remedy for disaster. To call them neo-pagan may be too generous a term for the lunatic liberal who has made this paradise into a polyglot pandemonium compromise with Lucifer.

To divorce pure freedom as the essence of God and world's greatest restraining force through his word of one, everything once considered good becomes evils chaotic hell. Nothing of an objective fire annealed word of matter or its math can reverse the plaque. When prayer and bible reading exited education and the public forum hate had no moral restraining force, not only did drugs, sex, and rock and roll quietly fill the vacuum but even worse was to see children return to kill their fellow classmates.

In this new civil law arena who can ever forget Columbine, Newtown, Parkland High, the Amish school and many others plus mass shootings of police, synagogues, churches, concerts and private clubs. The angel of death was now loosed to choose the venue at will to inflict its horror of vicious murder or drug and vaping overdose. The words evil and sin remained dormant to protect political correctness and insure social justice to the perpetrator. The liberal fanatic still blamed the gun and mental state for the tragedy but never the evisceration of the invincible word of one from education and the public forum. No blame for the pagan liberation that abrogate the sacred honor of our founding principles that inspired and blessed this nation unlike any other in the world.

No fact of a dismal science or liberal advocate can deny that the same power of the word that created the secondary heaven and earth, sent the plaques, healed the sick, rose the dead, or filled the prophets with its spirit, was any less powerful, when read over a public address system by a loving child each morning.

This may be our last chance as a sovereign nation to strike back at a liberal demon-crat scoundrel who welcomed the extrication of God's word and the piercing of His sacred womb of life. Our inspired freedom sovereign Christian enlightened roots still shed insight into this reprobate whose genesis out of fiery evil sanctioned slavery, Jim Crow, segregation, overturning of abortion restrictions, removal of prayer and bible reading, same sex marriage, transgenderism, appeasement and buying off our enemies. They gave us the hoax of fossil fuel, global warming, gun confiscation, the death of natural law, hatred for capitalism, our founders, the Jew, and the irrational thought of living side by side with terrorism, evil empires, sanctuary cities, a burgeoning bureaucracy and a Marxist socialist transformation. And let us not forget who put an end to the Monroe Doctrine or the Panama Canal that now has China, Russia and Iran at our doorstep.

Now we see how they could lose an election then by a phony dossier scheme of collusion and the lie impeach a lawfully elected president on a joke and his extolling of their crimes. Finally after a flimflam zombie sham and lie filled impeachment of the president, to observe their antics in the State of the Union address as they sat like inbred Caesars, impotent, cold, caged and evil.

In summary, is the sad irony that unbeknownst to the entire populous, these socialists' demons are using fake civil law to impeach not only the president, but the constitution, the Declaration of Independence, and pure freedom of our inspired God. They, if successful, would have impeached every principle of a people's republic that respects life, liberty, property ownership of weapons and the pursuit of freedoms happiness. This upcoming election may be our last chance to purge the demon-crat hundred year united front destruction of capitalism. These fools deserve to be ostracized and their socialist dreams placed in limbo alongside their loathing press.

SENSE-ESSENCE AND NONSENSE

America, we have a problem on the periphery. One is a dawning of a Golden Age, while in the other a colossal trial of the Republic is brewing unlike ever before. Similar to the hollow seashell held against the ear we wonder is it the flood of the sea or is it a turmoil of the blood that is about to erupt. There is a dementia unfolding which harkens to President Lincoln who predicted that America could only be destroyed from within.

So let me ask, after God's sifting of the Jew, the gentile and pagan for his Eden II founding has it come for naught beneath our feet that we have succumbed to the shame of a glorified mission. If not the living, who must first ask of the pagan ancestry the traits that mold the liberal hedonist warrior mentality, that was divorced from the soils instruction, or was the problem a congenital condition of birth that occurred when the mother as God's earthly moralizer was jarred from the home as a spoil of war.

Was it not barbaric to believe she could be replaced of her moral duty by an animated, insensate, amoral transistorized improvisation? Surely, a public education was a disaster at harvesting the ethical principles of good via the abstract objective chaff of sense. To never teach the all-powerful absolute word of plus and minus one as not only the miracle of the atom but the negative electrifying word of God that generate a cosmos with a numbered essence of quality each coded for our earthly mission. As such by electron magic the God of creation was ever present in every cell of our being. Should I ask, knowing they communicate with one another, do they ever complain of being lonely?

Unfortunately, the word essence was too spiritual to cross the threshold of education leaving the vital soul to metamorphose in fire. Wasn't it amazing that from the absolute word of one we were bestowed negative charged essence as the word of God made real in pure freedom guided by natural law then ordained to our founders to safeguard alongside its moralizing Christian truths of the beloved constitution. Electron ionized essence, the vital constituent of all things of existence, lies dormant behind the demented demon-crat madness and their baseless, non-criminal impeachment. Even though when Pasteur first discovered its concentrated spirit in alcohol, be termed it the "essence of life."

For many students their vague knowledge of electron essence is for its distilled sedating of the euphoric senses after a week of abstract frustration, the same for the hallucinogenic drug and its vaping companion. Ever wonder why one in four consider suicide?

The essence of God is freedom, unity, oneness, wholeness, completeness, and perfection the absolute and together love. As darkness is the essence of light, and of life the reasoning soul, how often does the beautiful aroma of the flower remind us of the essence of its miracle seed? Fire is one of the most diverse whose essence is as a useful servant and most frightful master. Finally, as for the psychopath Bolshevik demon-crat out to transform the greatest economic and political system ever, their essence is demonic power.

America, as an appendage and scapegoat of the crucifixion was doubly blessed by the essence of freedom in unity with the moral essence of Christianity. Matter abounds in the subjective qualify of essence which gives it a unique character of specified atom combinations whose mathematical numbered essence is proven by the human DNA miracle. This infinite coded essence is a result of the transmuted word of the 107 electron generated atoms which will pollinate and cross-pollinate into ubiquitous variety of beauty and excellence.

We live in a parallel universe of matter and spirit, positive and negative, night and day, summer and winter, subject and object, living and dying, sense and essence, good and evil, etc. ours is the image world with no truths or absolutes except by faith to decipher the pathos and power of the absolute word of one. From the word of one we have a positive and negative atom generated universe.

KNOW THYSELF

This pearl of wisdom, and most important advice, ever given to one who trod on earth is engraved on the Oracle of Delphi in Ancient Greece. Great teachers and conscious souls like Attic Solon and St. Augustine who led England to Christian conversion, believed "to know thyself" was the first law of human nature. Search your memory for the teacher who used this phrase as a course objective and pillar of a conflicting mental duality. The answer is none and of wasted resource, how many students will seek the drug or narcotic to numb the senses and soothe the neglected haunt.

Had the DNA discovery been recognized as an inspired code for human motivational excellence and not for its hucksters to use as a road map from whence, but as a guiding light to the bloom and success of the wither. Should we wonder why because it meant deference to God only five percent of the DNA is productive while ninety five percent lies dormant?

The DNA miracle sculpture which should have been the most revered and entrancing ever revealed by God was discovered in 1953 by two scientists J. D. Watson and F. H. Crick. This double stand plus and minus word of one hydrogen macro molecule coded miracle of each individuals embryonic growth and potential was akin to discovery of the Holy Grail cup of divine power.

Why was it downplayed as the most entrancing and elegant gift of God the answer is simple; what should we expect from an agnostic, non-believing atheist who denies a supreme being as having credit for how it got into the human gene? We must believe that this revelatory secret was presented to man just prior to the removal of His holy word from education before being thrown onto the laps of hell as a feverish plea of sanity.

WHERE AMERICA WENT WRONG

As mentioned earlier this is not the America of its founding nor are we its people, the founders, nor its constitution and declaration of rights. Although in our hearts America represents an ideal not of man but by God and that too is a travesty. Not accustomed by our ancestry to fashion our belief on the dual aspects of a heaven and hell unity led us to follow the object and ignore a unity with the spirit. As such it would be the foolish and corruptible we would choose believing we were wise while God would use the mighty of miracles to confound the foolish. Even the time worn adage "In God We Trust" overtime became absent in spirit and nothing above its dictation.

Had we trust in God as an eternal mission then the two greatest manifestations of our genesis were those of freedom and its moralizing Judea-Christian ethic. A dual creation gave us a dual language one of object christened in fire and another subjective pure in essential quality.

Under the old Satan deluder act our early instruction followed scripture in avoidance of the corruptible. Pure freedom as the essence of God was quickly converted as not of the antithesis of immorality but a man invented word to make compromise with evil. This would eventually lead to the abrogation of God from education and the public forum. Should we wonder how this act alone will breed a liberal reformer bent on stripping the constitution of its encapsulated moral mosaic laws?

Unless American education can be transformed to teach the non-religious fundamentals of absolute one as it would become the positive and negative matrix of the miracle atom the future is bleak. Whereas plus one refers to corruptible matter and negative one is the mathematics of infinite purity, energy and trans-mutational power. To ignore it and its generative wave responsible for all form and function was suicidal, mainly because it is the ionizer of the imperishable soul which has custody over the depraved body. Rather than rely on a cradle to grave health care drug that masks the problem, take heed to the most superhuman healing power on earth.

One of the great mistakes of the liberal neo-pagan was not to teach the duality of a heaven and earth unity, yet unity of opposites towered over the compromise with evil. With that in mind America will lose favor with God when, as a spoil of war the mother, as God's earthly representative, is jarred from the home and replaced by an insensate, amoral glass eye. This could not happen unless by hijack of the electron negative wave, the miracle medium of divine essence is made a transport system for hells most vile and morally debased. In an earlier time the mother as God's representative, would have buffered such liberal and demonic nonsense.

With all the moral mooring the inspired founders and evangels of the cross went through to bring God's gift, through the Jew of monotheism, to our shores was it too much to ask of every immigrant? An assimilation of the language and our traditional belief in God's freedom inspired Judea-Christian enlightenment. Neither of which by natural truth are a religion. The fact that Christianity will become the anchor pin for denominational religious creeds was a manifestation of freedom sifting a nation of believers in His Sovereign Son's birth, death and resurrection. To me that is no different than charging the many tongues to accept the English language as a condition of settlement, or of Christianity and the inspired constitution.

Again, it boils down to a mind over matter pride in our spiritual or a matter over mind hedonism that from their pockets of foreign identity have hate for God, Christianity, the Jew, the constitution, etc. No one should be given a free pass just to get on the proverbial liberal dole.

The reason why hell has become a non-sequitur of education is because the vital soul is a cryptic and ambiguous mystery as custodian over all of creation including the human body. Just because it did not meet pagan tangible standard as being real they chose to praise the devil and shame God.

In Jewish ancient tradition the "Azazel" angel of death or young bull scapegoat of the temple that was released into the wilderness, must return to separate the soul from the body. We know the body returns to dust and the American scapegoat return to assist Israel in the tribulation. That may sound like a stretch but not when considering an eternal soul as the moral custodian over all of creation. Eternity is about purity in its most infinite quantum whereby it leads us in a multiplicity of services of unending oracle to oracle.

When Christianity died we became thoughtless and thankless in a new ethic called political correctness which persecutes the mind to turn the other cheek that was just what the capitalist liberal subversives wanted. So while our sacred treasure was fighting for freedom abroad and warriors returning painfully broken and mangled of limb and mind we often forgot for what they toiled, and the nations eternal spirit wounded as well. By God, their effort was not in vain. President Trump was freedoms eternal favor to beguile the liberal loons in their misleading deceptive and fraudulent grimy behavior against God and country. Anyone who has any perception of reason must realize that every stone they threw at this man missed their mark.

Another malfunction of American greatness was to consider how under the font of freedoms God our precious warrior treasure was goaded to fight unending protracted wars abroad while at home the muscovite scoundrel was pillaging every institution and anarchical splinter group with capitalist hate. Was it because we took for granted that freedom, even of the vicarious and corruptible, was irresistible in its defense against evil. To associate pure freedom with hell and never educate the generations of its dual nature was criminal.

Freedom, as the essence and negative word of God, in unity with the soul of man, to never cross the threshold of education was to educate the stubble and worthless chaff of the ripened seed and discard the mainstay and staff of life.

Today, America is an empty tomb and the left leaning wing of congress a morbid sepulcher of bitter tongue aligned to transform the greatest economic and political system on earth. This may be our last election when an ignorant populous finally elects an old Bolshevik conman as a lead up to tribulation. So before you cast your pearls to the swine reflect on the Azazel angel of death of ancient Jewish tradition that must separate the soul from the body at death. We know the body is returned to dust but as for the soul neither the most beggarly nor erudite of knowledge knows with certitude its destiny.

For this reason alone, the never taught and least understood of Gods negative inspired generative wave, hold the secret of the departed soul. Even science admits the electron generative wave is a transverse undetected invincible that traverses to the depths of hell and back unimpeded and un-surveilled to it ethereal abode. Wouldn't it make sense that this is the transport line assigned to carry our noble deeds and resolute belief in His Son's birth, death and resurrection to an eternal bliss?

Since the beginning of time great philosophic minds have made note of the greatest need being to "know thyself", why? Because the rungs of the latter in this climb are planted in hells chaos and the upward rungs are fraught with ignorance. Once God and Christian morality are removed the climb becomes hells deadly bane and even nature lacks its imparting instruction. Nothing of life is more dreadful than to know the strong, wise and beautiful of godlike power stand mute always surrounded by the ugliness of sin and an education be damned.

When a nation so blessed with heavens purity and goodness runs out of honesty, love, beauty, virtue and justice they've also run out of the divine subjective essence that has put the worst of times ahead not behind. By any standard the vastness of creation is impossible for anyone soul to comprehend. However, every purposeful dispensation for each coded DNA waits to be fettered through channels only God understands with intricacy.

First, we must superimpose the Trinity of God's will above our every act to obtain a cellular wisdom that brings health and happiness to a full life. The mundane nonchalant cool and indifferent demeanor of soul is the prescription for an emptiness of body and mind.

Every child must know that our ostentatious neo-pagan schools only teach what is non-ethical and amoral of inert object never the subjective encyclopedia of negative purified essence. They should understand why God has shielded every truth from these scavengers of truth and obscured it with a miracle.

No other place on earth equaled that of an American God given freedom to visually and stereoscopically unify the universe of a transparent heaven into a oneness with an earthly material body. By never teaching nor focusing on this world of opposing contradictory extremes of a heaven and hell, positive and negative need for unity, set us apart like the titanic and the Carpathian passing in the shadow death of night into the divide of darkness and pain.

The following is a mental exercise and anchor pin for discovering self.

- Pretend you are standing in a vertical position feet together and hands down
- Next raise both arms skyward and together 180°
- Extend the left arm 90° outward horizontally
- Do the same with the right

Congrats; you have just formed the human sculpture of absolute one. The left arm represents positive charged earth whose essence is gravity. The opposing right arm represents the negative electron ionizing generation of Godly essence. In unity the negative of natural moral law should imbibe and take custody of the corruptible. Unity means wholeness, completeness, truth, absolute and uncompromising pure freedom. All are one as stated in the beginning introductory sentence of Holy Scripture.

Next take notice to a positive mathematics that can only progress by mind or digial speed of sound into matters conception in fire. Negative one retracts into the pure of infinity.

AN OXY-MORONIC UNIVERSE

For this critical narrative oxy means pure and God inspired, while moronic is matter related, fire annealed and an accomplice of hells definition of freedom. In real life they convert into miracles and madness. Never does a day pass without the moronic spirit of the dust, rally his accomplice man, to destroy the oxy-pure freedom inspired soul. Don't underestimate the influence of the moronic as it has evolved since confrontation in Eden I. Since the fifteenth century renaissance, a moronic affront to the rising tide of Christianity, through the likes of Darwin, Freud and Marx was festooned to the new found atheistic icon of science. An obsession with earth's delusionary imperfect mathematical "fact" made it the perfect accomplice. First, there is no such thing as science. There are only improvisational sciences that dignify every aspect of a material culture. The only true science like true freedom is of creation that exudes in natural law, perpetual miracle and is impervious to factual truth. That leaves the impostors of science all about half-truths and all lies.

After six centuries of fire annealed objective probes they still lack any truth of the what, who, why or how of any causal miracle. Their rise to fame began when Galileo first discovered that gravity was the reason why things fall to earth. But as for the truth of what is gravity, light, water, air, earth, the electron, atom, universe, electricity, God or any of the billions of causal truth everything is speculative. As a result their bailiwick has been to undress the nomenclature of things and present it for rote memorization and exploratory study. This has been most beneficial for the medical, biological and various sciences. Missing from this laborious kettle of fish is their failure to unify the how of things with the oxy-pure of the essence responsible for the form, function, character, personality and potential that exists in every cell of matters being. Unfortunately in this dual creation of imperfect sense and pure eternal essence, because no charred fact of imperfect math can explain what is God, his essence is ignored. Although, not fully as it surfaces in a retributive way on the agenda of the modern school. It outcrops as a reserve for a Friday night euphoria where the essence of fermented grain dulls a week of frustrated mush laden anxiety.

When Pasteur first discovered alcohol he thought he had discovered the essence of life. Someday belatedly we might all sense what it is that gives the beautiful flower its distinct aroma or the charming face its attractive glance and cheerful smile. The truth of essence lies hidden in the scriptural instruction guide to wisdom. It used to grace our schools and places of overnight lodging but for a single moronic mind and liberal judgeship the guarding angels of the constitution had no national advocate of defense. As a result the introductory prologue for a life of heavenly essence here and beyond lies with Dante's' divine comedy promises of hell or purgatory.

For those of a matter monism pause while I introduce you to the most beautiful of essence that explains the origin of human knowledge. It begins by stating: "in the beginning was the word and the word was one in God." We, the moronic orphans of an engineered scientific lie should not be alarmed to learn that this creative miracle of which we are its ancillary of the word of one, has been brutalized and removed from the dissemination of knowledge. Ever since the infamous court banned the miracle word of one in prayer and bible reading the steady implosion of Gods Eden II America is nearing its climax. When children return to their classroom to kill their own living ancillary of the miracle word blame rests not with the inanimate weapon.

Unlike our mentor Israel from which the seed of a monotheistic God gave birth, their government has defended the traditional religious belief of customs throughout the ages. While under Roman rule and their rejection of Christ Israel paved the way for America to become the divine sanctuary for a freedom enlightened Christian inspired paradise. Just as there is no word to describe the concept of God, or his miracle word of one, this Trinity should have been exalted and revered as the most essential and fundamental quality of human existence. Every miracle that expired on the dreadful cross was resurrect to lay waste its Roman crucifiers and by assimilating soul follow freedoms faithful out of paganistic tyranny and oppression to nestle in America. God surely knew how fragile that honor was for there was skepticism with the Gentile knowing that Christ only sent one apostle to minister to them. Now we know why as we have watched their freedom inspired empire implode from a reversion to their immoral neo-pagan beliefs. For what is more pagan then to annul a beginning and replace it with an evolved state of gas and dust that arose to perfection like the legendary Phoenix from the ashes of hell. Or that man evolved as the fittest of animal by phony natural selection.

By eliminating a dual heaven and hell creation allowed the atom to be claimed as all matter absent the electron spirit ionizing wave as the generator of all existence. Light will be caused by matter bombarding matter particles and "Big Bang" will become the pagan deity to surmount Gods vacated throne. Has time arrived to realize that this creative miracle of the divine word of one that made us junior gods of nature, has been brutalized and bastardized beyond reproach. Ever since that infamous liberal decision banned the essence of prayer and bible reading the implosion from within of Gods Eden II miracle in freedom appeared imminent. Once the veil of heaven was removed from knowledge the culture turned rancid in illicit sex, drugs, abortion of millions, loss of hope, open borders, terrorism and a polarized libertine loss of values. Under the radar thousands of our industry its wealth and intellectual technological genius became scattered among our enemies depleting the nation's industrial base. An economic tsunami will further burden the country with ill-conceived massive bailouts, welfare bonanzas, inane printing of unbacked fiat, and socialist cradle to grave health care with a debt of cascading infinitude.

In this murky "God is dead" setting splinter groups began an open season killing of police with a sinister yet convoluted unnamed cause. In the midst of a political firestorm students began killing other innocent students wantonnessly as a premonition the genie had finally escaped its evil vial. Should we ask, if so is this the prelude to the chapter never taught of the dreaded anti-Christ deceptor. If so are there portents of his likeness saliently concealed in that touch pad mysticism we admire. Thankfully, amidst such profane hyperbole, an eternal numbered essence has not faltered in its resolve of miracle for everyday convenience. Unfortunately that universe of essence lies dormant. Our only hope hinges on November 3rd of 2020 and its advent of a new beginning that gives renewed focus on our moronic citadels of learning. Never was the hour more critical for the uniting of moronic sense and inspired essence into a oneness of truth. If we have learned one lesson from the most damaging and damning administration ever is that the swords of the Caesars have now been sheathed, hopefully forever. And with it the moronic spirit that led to banishment in Eden I then metastasize to mastermind the crucifixion in century one and now poised in 21 to declare victory over freedom, the essence of God. God bless heavens man of the hour to stand firm. His desire is to make America superior and great not for conquest, but for other nations to emulate.

When the universe was cast as a binary phenomenon of oxy-moronic extremes, man also was of necessity bequeathed the gift of dual choice, a free will over which only man had full control. God knew that sense alone could not suffice to answer the whence whither, when and how of truth. This required a free will aligned to both the real of things as well as the ability to transcend the ideal to revel in the infinite miracles concealed for faith only. This single benevolent act created a catch 22 for God who had no choice but to watch and wait.

All of us came into this world as oxy-morons. This simply means that as dual beings we are composed of the diametric extremes of positive charged matter and negative essence in need of unity. As a seed universe whose genesis is of a heaven and earth composition unless both are fused in oneness then life becomes a crap-shoot. At birth the mother assumes the role of God to stabilize and complete the miracle of transformation. If our schools can't do the same then close them down, pay off the debt and start over with the old Satan Deluder Act that made us great. Once these preliminaries are met the juggernaut occurs in stage two when the role of education is to fortify the child's unity to the oxy-pure, not to direct a child's sense of being towards the inert and imperfect of a material mooring.

According to natural law that bond is fortified between the positive of matter and the negative of essence into the miracle of perfection. It was for mankind to adopt the secret which is not of nature's doing, but of a supernatural prime-mover of trans-mutational power of the word. Therefore by natural law when diametric extremes face one another as contradictory opposites the one most pure, virtuous and moral must imbibe and take custody of the other. It was precisely for this reason that earthly matter was conceived in a state of fiery hell to insure it would forever be of imperfect, amoral quantity. That includes the language and mathematics which could only become of excellence by fusion with the pure of essence. Everything of creative excellence exudes of spirit essence that gives the matter embryo its distinct form, function and potential. If you don't believe this know that at our disposal is a total abandoned encyclopedic of pure, matter less, objectiveless words to aid in the transformation such as; truth, beauty, love, life, light, air, fire, water, atom, color freedom, wisdom, knowledge, consciences, sense, gravity, electricity, etc., etc.

To call someone an oxy-moron is like telling a friend they are beautiful and ugly or cruel and kind, smart but dumb, etc. Does not nature gleam of the true and false, living and dying, happy and sad, beautiful and ugly? And do we not all exhibit the split-personality of both saint and sinner?

Absent the diametric extremes of attracting and repelling, positive charged gravity and negative electricity there could be no existence of anything. We are passengers on a motionless rotating and revolving miracle carousel, where propulsion outward and interdependent bodies attracting inward, unless internally balanced could become madness. That is why in every atom except hydrogen, which was the first on a one to one basis between the proton and electron, all remaining 106 offspring have an internal neutron balancing stem. Duality of opposites requires unity of balance. Unfortunately, science refuses to accept the principle and natural law of duality for a mechanical unilineal hypothesis for cause and effect, thus eliminating any external spiritual factor, thus causing the American experiment of Gods natural laws to be expunged for man's civil law of an infirmed freedom. This will remove the balance stem of unity between an oxy-moronic congress that will turn the soul of a freedom inspired government into a modern day den of madness. On one side of the isle sits the left hand of God represented by the proton matter embryo and on the opposite, the right hand, dedicated to the natural laws embodied in the sacred constitution. Because the left sides of the atom creation is energized by the essence of the right hand required unity of difference in oneness of freedom. Unfortunately, when the age of science aborted natural law for the mundane of civil the word essence will be removed from knowledge. Sense without the oxy-pure of essence will bisect heaven from earth allowing for chaos to return.

All of us know what sense is. Our bodies have the ability to see, hear, touch, taste, feel, etc. all are not primarily for sensual pleasure of a civil law freedom, but because of light and a transparent atmosphere able to revel in the fathomless miracles of creation. Missing from this amazing world of the opposites of heaven and hell, good and evil, love and hate, man and woman, night and day, light and darkness, sickness and health, etc. are the opposites of sense and essence.

No child will have essence explained as that which gives everything its uniqueness of character, personality and delightful appearance. To ask where that great reservoir of essence exists that gives the flower its special fragrance we know it is not on earth. It does however come from the electron inspired side of the atom.

Our instruction guide explains its origin in its very first line that; "in the beginning was the word and the word was the essence of God." From the word, by infinite negative purity of number it will make its way into every atom building block of existence.

Nature is not God. It is however the essence and word of God. You and I are nature, yet we are not God. His essence lies within every cell of our being and the soul is its repository that commands the mind and the body. When we consider that nature was created out of chaos there had to be a starter of the first start to turn chaos into the miracle of a seed perfection.

Three things are necessary for anything to exist. First is a planner and a plan, how the plan is executed and thirdly the security of the execution. Only one means exists that goes from the concept to the working model absent the trial and error fundamentals and that is by transubstantiation of the word. The concept is pure, it is powerful and it is miraculous. It was witnessed on earth with the raising of the dead, the driving out of spirits, healing of the sick, the blind, the leper and the changing of water into wine. Then there were the two fishes and five loaves that fed five thousand with twelve baskets to spare plus many never recorded.

For the moronic among us of the endangered self-righteous they prefer the instant magic of the touch screen which is not a miracle but a transmutation of images via the electron spirit wave we call electricity. Should this transverse wave that generates an entire universe ever cease then in the twinkling of an eye darkness and chaos returns. Should this happen and all of nature succumb only then will those who worship nature as God, realize how wrong they were. For this reason, great concern exists that a rogue state by exploding a nuclear bomb high above earth damaging the electron generative wave will turn earth into darkened void. Thank God our new president was moved to recognize the threat and not follow the appeasement policies of the past. Never are the words oxy-moron more haunting and distressful than when an American spiritual enlightenment is faced with a rash of bloodletting school tragedies. One report claims that since 2013 there have been three hundred killing sprees. If there was only one that takes us back to Columbine or the Amish school and then Sandy Hook tells us something is dreadfully wrong. And to castigate blame on the weapon, the NRA or the Second Amendment is equally wrong.

Once a child of God is taken from the sacred womb and nurtured or the annealed word of inert matter for an abstract grade devoid of an ethic we have as a people placed an innocent miracle in search of truth into opulent liers of lone distraction. Studies reveal that one in four children consider suicide. Objective matter alone is inert, amoral and a frustrating aggregate in need of essential refinement. When the essence of prayer and bible reading were banned with it went the mooring of the good, the true and the beautiful. Absent the power of the word may well be the reason why our schools since 1963 have become such killing fields by childhood madness. We can compare the refinement or fusion process to the forty-niners who after exhausting their search for gold in California entered Nevada. After unearthing tons of seemingly worthless black ore their bitter disappointment was to learn it would become the famous Comstock silver lode to be worth billions. If silver like most minerals are amalgams with other metals are we not human amalgams in need of moral refinement with the oxy-pure? These are miracle prodigies sent for refinement and we have been hoodwinked to believe that meant preparing them for a financial career. What a shame to believe money and matter can replace a foundational belief that all blessings emanate from the goodness of God. America has been woefully deceived by the lie that freedom is not the essence of God but a man inspired phenomenon of godlike power. Not until Christianity was borne of the cross was America destined as the miracle of a united oneness. By furloughing our most salient human need to the vultures of a liberal united front bent on destruction of God, Christianity and the conventional traditions of our founding was criminal. As we must live with the tragedies of innocent childhood death know that those heinous killings is not the fault of the Second Amendment but rests solely on the bloodletting soul of those who divorced the spirit of God from those innocent miracles of creation.

For the grieving families and a nation who responds by asking: how could God allow such calamity to happen, the answer is resounding; God has been surgically removed from this moronic paradise by an atheistic science and liberal united front of which a majority is their vassal.

When school prayer and bible reading was removed the invisible power of the oxy-pure ceased in extending the benevolence of security and understanding. Another name for the ubiquity of miracles is a gift bestowed as a blessing from God. Miracles are Gods favor of praise to enlighten the soul through his grace of knowledge.

The ignoble liberal atheist who placed matter over mind not only was allowed to annul the pure universe of divine blessing but to turn modern education into palatial edifices of abstract stud-farm relevance. A blatant matter directed ontology has condemned to ruin the family, the farm, the soil, the offspring, an environment of everything good and virtuous along with the soul of a people and the nation. As an epoch of madness was overtaking a backdrop of miracles our honorable police were being slaughtered indiscriminate as was life in the sacred womb and with it the classroom. We know now whose blood of the police is on those hands. As death was overtaking life the moronic loon still castigate blame on the gun, the NRA and the Second Amendment. These were phantoms of the illusion that money and laws could save the republic – a scotoma of the perverted soul blind them to an America made great by the homage our fathers made requisite to the God of our destiny.

Nothing bears the title of oxy-moronic more than the dual creation of a heaven and hell unity. Never should a day pass without fascination of that miracle bond of diametric extremes into a perfection of unified oneness. In the human sphere that challenge of will is omnipresent and much to popular chagrin money is not a bonding or unifying agent. For our schools to focus the dissemination of an objective twelve year syllabus of knowledge, towards a financial career absent the unifying principle of freedom was barbaric. The axis of man, not unlike the flowering seed requires the transforming light to reach excellence of maturity. Our greatest challenge after ripening in the sacred womb is to detour that part of the moronic self that keeps transforming the spirit of the dust into an angel of light. In the annals of time, the American anthology is one of the most unique as the freedom inspired hemisphere to propagate the soul of mankind safely through the dual hostile empires of light and darkness. We have failed in this regard to tame the free will in the truth of knowledge, just as fire is most useful for the advent of light. This reminder cannot be overstressed on two fronts. First, before man came to be, freedom was the essence of God. Second and equally just, because Israel was, America came to be. Together, in this critical epoch of incredulous enmity freedom is preparing the chess board for the hurling of the millstone against those who corrupted his word of truth. America, under its newly sanctified neophytes, Moses and Aaron (although miracle workers on the economic front), is not for a life of ease. They have taken on this high honor, not of their own accord but by freedoms calling. Just as Israel's great prophets and leaders were not called by their own account, America has now reached the crossroads where like the withering rose attached to the virgin thorn – we have become the withering thorn on the bloodstained rose. Unless we can break free to feed on prayer for ourselves and for our appendage Israel, freedoms chasm of evil will only grow darker on the moronic thorns of liberal assassins.

Today America is morally and financially bankrupt and even with the ascension of a resurrected Moses to lead a people out of bondage a hedonistic detestation infects his Godly mission. Akin to the Pharisee, Sadducees and scribes of old even the righteous suffering death and resurrection of the cross did not deter their liberal madness.

Only one simple solution prevented American demise and it was bequeathed by freedom as the only revealed truth for fulfillment of his prototype heaven on earth. Its answer resides in the following Trinity. All are bound in oneness of letter A.

A1	A2	A3
God's plan of creation The atom	The crucifixion of Christ	The pouring out of the Spirit to mankind

There was something about the gentiles of the west that made us aloof of the lessons history revealed of the vanquished past. We preferred to become the reformed neo-pagans of a scientific equalitarianism based on the false facts of natural pride. No fact taught that Roman demise occurred because of pagan belief which of necessity sowed the seed of Christianity.

America is a very special nation, not because of its brotherly affection or economic prowess, but because of its divine mission by an inspired people. Like Israel, our ordained appendage, whose trust was in a monotheistic God of creation made us illuminaries of a religious enlightenment. As with Israel, God is ever mindful of our mission. As early as 500 BC, the genius of Plato regarded God as the measure of all things. The beginning, middle and end all, containing in himself the true essence of all things. He saw God as the unifier between the ideal of essence and the real of sense. Many regard Plato as bringing heaven to earth so man could better ascend to heaven.

A thousand years hence an atheistic science will lay claim that man is the measure of all things. They like Aristotle will question how ideas and lifeless number can have a desire or longing. Their lame idea was that by some law of mechanics all things evolved out of nothingness. How was such a law, by whose miracle was it formulate as to arrive at perfection by act of happenstance? Further, their claim, if it can't be explained drive the idea of its truth out of mind. This underlies the existential theory of modern education and belies why the elements tender of rage in advance of a "scattering" or something worse.

For this narrative the crucifixion has proven that not only can transition occur from the ideal to the sensible but as well from the sensible to the ideal as Christ has made witness. The DNA miracle handprint in the human gene further proves how lifeless number is really a miracle implanted code that directs every human function from embryonic growth in form, personality, physical expression and potential. No better example exists of the essence of what love of God means. What makes this narrative so heart-wrenching and sad is that the greatest nation on the face of the earth, as a God inspired freedom, has already been conquered by a one-dimensional, unilinear, mechanical existential demon of the dust villain.

THE TRANSFORMATION

This world envy of oxy-pure transformation first occurred in 1620 at Plymouth Rock, with the signing of a covenant for self-government. Signed by the defenders of Christian faith "in the name of God, Amen," this revered signing of visionary pilgrims is a date that should live in timeless and prayerful honor.

The second glorious of oxy-pure would occur in 1776 with the signing of the immortal Declaration of Independence. Concurrent was the miracle of the atoned Adam now given a last name Smith to present our founders with the greatest book every written to foster an individual incentivized economic and political blueprint for administering Gods Eden II provisional paradise. I lived through that Golden Age whose doctrine of the invisible hand of competition wed to a freedom inspired regulation of supply, demand and price and a love for God built the greatest nation on the face of earth.

Before his death Adam Smith, one of the great professors of moral sentiments, would order all of his pontifical philosophy to be burned, yet his influence has never been equaled on political and economic philosophy. Two reasons come to mind as to why. First, he foresaw that the evils of a liberal atheistic greed would refuse to unify and accept the outcome of competition and instead would seek to slay their competitor giving way to monopolies, trusts, cartels, interlocking directorates and massive government regulation and taxation. Second, he still held visions of Eden one and the brutal treatment his master suffered on the cross thus relinquishing all hope that his efforts could save the American ideal. That brings us to the bitter united front evil transformation that began in 1963 with the annulment of God and Christianity as the death knell to freedom and prosperity.

Someday, if there are honest future historians they will record this date, not as a victory for human rights but a "scattering" of Gods blessings in industry, jobs, intellectual inventive knowledge, a balance of trade and finance, and protective shield in super power world status.

We must believe that President Trump and Vice President Pence were a blessing of unexplained miracle, not unlike Moses and Aaron, sent to lead this nation back to its sacred roots. For those who say we can't go back and that we must accept the sacrificing of the unborn to the deity Moloch, same sex marriage, transgender public accommodation, schools without a moral ethic, or the lewd and lascivious vile perversions via the sacred electron wave are dead wrong. If the God of freedom could sift the Tea Party patriot foot soldier to purge every branch of the Federal government and the majority of the state offices; they can do it for the cause of life with the proper motivation. Don't take my word go by the signs and its wonders made present by the miracle ellipse followed by the worst hurricanes ever and the scorching fires. Or do we prefer a forty to one, as the Israelis suffered after losing trust in God? Let us heed the warning and save the dread of evil trembling.

This man of steel who successfully followed his guiding light through the parted sea of scandalous fire, once on holy ground he veered left and turned aside a liberal appointee and placed an originalist onto the nation's highest court. Immediately he turned right and repealed the hated Johnson Act that hamstrung pastors from their freedom of religion, then in deference to God he renewed American solidarity with Israel who was dastardly shunned for eight years. On the economic side it was nothing short of a miracle as the prodigal son of a freedom inspired proclamation began returning their factories and wealth home after being scattered by moronic high taxes and crippling regulation.

As the economy returns this man of God must make a full frontal assault to return education, come hell or high water, back to its blessed roots where prayer and bible reading preempt daily classes. Abolish the Department of Education and return this reserved power to the states where the founders meant it to be. Next rein in the NEA which is an arm of the Democratic liberal party which funnels billions in dues not to enhance education but to fund party candidates.

Even more damaging that the Johnson Act is the scam called separation of church and state. Neither the word God, essence, nor absolute one have connotation to a religious preference. Both are necessary to bring sanity to a total objective syllabus of abstract ethical nothingness. If religion is a problem then invoke the oath to every teacher as I had to take upon being hired. Because of a communist threat well into the 1950's required me to take an oath that "I am not now, nor ever have been, a member of the Communist Party". That oath proved worthless as the united front was successful in infiltrating and corrupting every freedom inspired virtue of a good people. If we need a religious oath then why not, "I will not in my teaching career advocate any religious preference as part of my dissemination of any and all subject matter."

Exactly one hundred years ago in 1917, when the Bolsheviks seized power in Russia, they saw capitalism whose faith lay in the Adam Smith private property ownership of wealth, as the sole enemy of communism. They believed that inequality of wealth was the cause for equality of poverty. When the class struggle among the capitalists did not produce revolts they devised a plan to destroy capitalism internally by the popular front or united front principle. That plan simply meant their followers must join any organization or disgruntled group to bring the system down.

In the old days the Russian was considered as someone who knew nothing; cared to know nothing and cared not that anything was worth knowing. Well fools, take that falsehood and plaster it on lady liberty's pedestal as the most snookered by the deceptive Russian bear in the history of the world.

Everyone on the demon-crat witch-hunt should be in jumpsuits and carted off for invoking the claim of false guilt, when the entire country and its institutions have been pillaged and bastardized by the sleaze bags of a liberal united front. You're damn right they've interfered in our elections and why not, they're in everything else, to the point that the only thing not steeped in atheistic, socialist dogma is the ability to appeal before freedom and with penitent heart cry out; My God, my God! Why have we forsaken thee!

Chalk it up as a spoil of WWII when they were our ally and with victory our guard was down. We knew they had infiltrated when in 1919 with the "Red Scare" many were tried and deported. Then in 1950 the McCarthy committee hearings involving an alleged 205 communist infiltrators in the State Department proved to be questionable overreach. Two years hence the atomic bomb secrets will be passed by the Rosenberg traitors to the Russian spy. Each culprit when they met had a half section of a Jell-O box and upon meeting each presented his half of a surgical puzzle which shows the stupidity of a mastermind, right? Although the American traitors will suffer execution fast-forward a mere half century and ask yourself who and by what stealth of secrets built the Soviet arsenal of competitive might. And don't stop there, venture also into China, Iran and North Korea and ask the same question. Don't castigate freedom with the blame because that too she was raped along with Christianity that has made us a cesspool and immoral swamp steeped in moral turpitude. Then to top it off we elect a muscovite Caesar Adonis who has the Gaul to blame America for the troubles of the world.

As Marx and Engles believed from the beginning, the way to victory was by catering to the trade union base. Start with the teachers union or the AFLCIO and many others and follow the money and the political label they wear. Billions in union dues will favor the party whose liberal agenda has nurtured the universities staffed with anti-capitalist professorships in the political, legal and journalistic disciplines. Should we question why a former executive Adonis would grovel at the constitution as being too negative in its restraints? As if to say the removal of prayer and bible reading and the commandments of Christianity from the public forum, or the granting of wholesale abortions and same sex marriage were necessary reforms of an evil constitution.

In a mere half century these clandestine leaches with hatred for God and his divine essence, have by sense of fact destroyed natural law paving the road to tyranny. What began as separation of church and state has now made impotent and ineffectual this nations heritage to God, Christianity, pure freedom, commandments of the constitution and its natural laws of justice. Never have we become so polarized as to witness a State of the Union address and watch acolytes of government writhe in disgust when the words patriotism, liberty, God, prayer, the flag, national anthem, private property, chain migration, the constitution, Bill of Rights and Christianity are mentioned.

It is for this reason why the newly inducted and despised Moses has been transitioned from the ideal to the sensible as freedoms man of steel for the hour. As you read what has never been taught, know that freedom as the essence of God exists in every cell of our being. As such nothing occurs without his advocacy or for those uninspired an opposing advocate is ready made. As the nation recently listened to one of the most uplifting and miraculous economic revivals in the past decade, it was pathetic to watch what looked like the predacious Tasmanian Devils at a Holy Roller convention. These were portents of a coming epoch of robotic mind which science claims will be ten thousand times smarter, battery operated and miserably constipated. One in particular appeared to be an advance model for as mount Rush was quick to notice, a contusion of the robotic jaw causing the dentures to become mobile and erratic. Until science returns God to his righteous throne and sends Big Bang packing let's put on hold the robotic brain until we realize we have a serious endangered species problem that is fixate on a moronic flight into hell for all of us.

Today we abort the living seed and fascinate to the unproductive weed. The DNA with its fifty million or more bits of primary knowledge is estimated to be ninety-five percent unproductive of use. The remaining five percent has found its way into the crime labs for identification or for the sundry request to answer who we are. Unfortunately Ancestry dot com is a treasure trove for the criminal in search of vital statistics to commandeer old folks Social Security benefits or the like. I know because I was a victim. Of greater concern is the improvised spider's web used to attract its prey, now ionized as a hub for worldwide transfer of money and ideas at the speed of light. How amazing, divorced from the wisdom of the soil and seated in skyscraper cubicle, by the pulse of electron essence, nothing is any longer sacred or safe from pillage.

AMERICA UNDER SIEGE

My God, what this last administration has done that requires the new Moses to not only drain the liberal invenomous swamp but to exorcise every institution across the spectrum. With freedom as your guide you will not fail!

Whereby our spiritual mentor Israel was guided by the five prophetic books of the Pentateuch as her road map to destiny, America was inspired by the faith of the saviors crucified ill-gotten fate.

For two centuries the duality of his word saw a good people cordon off the treacheries of hell and fortify the soul with the righteousness of Christian belief. Unlike any nation in the world the oxy-pure blessings of freedom flowed. Miraculously, as we met the challenge to defend freedom throughout the world, to all its people we thought it could stand on its own merits at home.

How foolish not to learn from history and ignore with erring judgement Homers stratagem of advice for fools. The legend of the Trojan horse and the siege of Troy by Greece are believed to be both a legend and a nucleus of fact. As having relevance to the siege of America, instead of a horse, the term most apropos is in fact "the bear trap." This is the same bear that scripture refers to as Gog and Magog, the two nations led by Satan in the battle of Armageddon against the Kingdom of God.

As for the trap to snare the American fortress it predates to the end of World War II when Russia was our ally. After the surrender of Germany they refused to assist in the war in the pacific until after Japan had surrendered. I relate to this because General MacArthur, who understood Stalin's adamance at Potsdam and his demands to retake E. Europe, offered a plan to President Truman to lay siege the Russian army stationed in Manchuria. Of course Truman will reject the idea and fire MacArthur.

Next comes the decoy of protracted unfinished wars beginning with communist aggression in Korea, then Vietnam to drain American blood abroad while the United Front is busy raping the fabric of America at home. The verdict is now in and the freedom inspired Christian enlightened oxy-pure is blood stained and expiring before a moronic liberal paradox of ignorance.

As every commandment of Moses has now been shred in our covenant and a government and legal system concurs what remains of the damnable calumny is our destined role to rid the revealed calamity facing our trusted mentor. Her seventieth anniversary as a nation is another of fortuitous seven that may have revered meaning.

This being a heaven and hell conjointure of diametric extremes is insurance that any ignorance of combative siege is definitely not bliss. In the true sense negative charged heaven as the electrifying generator in conjunction with the positive ground of gravity makes matters hell by design, the cruel master of deathly siege.

Man, being the poster boy of positive matter frame and negative charged soul has in this bastion of liberating freedom been run amuck by the forces of darkness. Unfortunately, the antidote for this debilitating never ending conflict is focused on the drug, money and things. None however have an effective purifying effect whose travail leads to siege, chaos and eventual doom.

By natural design only one universal has the power to transform a people or nation from the bondage of antagonistic opposites. It was America's birthright as an Eden II paradise created by providence to join forces with an Israeli monotheism responsible for the advent of Christian inspired moralizing adjunct of freedom. Freedom as the most powerful force in the universe was first breathed to stem the convulsive hell of earths beginning, as well as set all cosmic form to perpetual motion. Never taught is that freedom is a restraining force not a liberating force of pent-up moral inhibitions. In a child's life it begins with the word no not yes. America could not become a bastion of Godly freedom until Christianity as its moralizing counterpart made its debut on the impaled cross of Christ. After barely two centuries these two Godparents of this freedom inspired paradise are now impaled as the vanquishers of human conflict and its siege of evil. America's franchise in freedoms moral light has been smitten by liberal Marxist materialist fools of political, legal, scientific, journalistic and educational slag.

Pause and reflect on what made America great before the advent of a digitalized logic. A computerized screen and its bombardment of the sense of sight has laid siege the once sacrosanct virtues of love, sex, truth, life, faith, marriage, soul, God, freedom and Christianity. Absent prayer and bible reading and diverting attention to the material visuals of sense has all but destroyed the oxy-pure of subjective reason and truth. These visuals most heinous and disdainful to the freedom inspired soul are pornography, drugs, sex and the morbid dismembering of the embryonic miracle seed of life. The greatest siege facing the latent honoree of freedoms mandate is not economic disparity but the age old enemy of ignorance. That ignorance failed to foresee a half century plus of vile Marxist united front, whose evil hatred for capitalism has its stamp of siege on every virtuous and hallowed relic of faith and honor in God's paradise. Once the visual fact of a deceptive science became the headmaster of a sterile indoctrinated education, the fix was ominous.

We can only imagine if a President Moses and a conservative court will return the miracles that part the sea, sent the plaques, healed the sick, changed water to wine, raised the dead, fed five thousand with five loaves and two fishes then with his transfiguration lay the plans for America.

That leaves us with the one siege reserved for the master planner that surpasses the knowledge of fact. Ask the imaginative soul if the elements of water, air, fire and earth know themselves? Don't answer hastily without considering that during rage the hurricane and typhoon reveal an eye, the tornado its vortex of destructive force, and the earthquake its convulsive furor. And by what act of conscious does the fluctuating jet stream high above earth steer the daily patterns of weather? Anyone who believes these are isolated acts of nature is ignorant of the power of the word of one. They reason not that America is by destiny a vision of both the real of object and ideal of subject bound by the natural laws of unity. Unity is God's plan for universal peace whose basis is to live by good or die to evil. Each of us exists in a perilous state of divided free will that demands unity of oneness in truth. Although never taught because unity reflects on the natural law of higher mathematics which states that in a world of opposites the one most virtuous must imbibe and take custody of the other. Examples include love having custody over hate, good over evil, health over sickness, heaven over earth, life over death, etc.

How strange that I resort to the nations famous battle of Gettysburg to draw similarity to the present siege of America's divinity in freedom. At Gettysburg two opposing armies one of the north and another of the south could have easily been given political labels of Democrat and Republican. If we add to that simile the democratic army will position its defenses on the right ridge called seminary and directly opposite the Republicans take a defensive left on cemetery ridge. Facing each other was a level plain where a three day battle raged that defies human description in the anomaly of brother against brother, region against region and ideal vs. ideal.

A century and a half later we watch as the fabric of the nation is again torn by the rancid thunder of an unholy unconditional surrender from the left bank of a political election skirmish. On the right under assault are the honest victors of constitutional law and election honesty. For the average Plebeian they were never educated to the fact that political correctness was a synonym of the united front ruse that a person of reason would call predatory conquering. In this bizarre case to undermine an election and complete the siege of capitalism and lay waste the nation. To be successful a liberal funded mania knowing innately they lacked the truth and savvy to impeach the businessman providential prodigy of freedom, mastermind a ploy of Roman anthology. After all if Pontius Pilate could find a way to impale the greatest miracle worker who ever walked the earth, why not a liberal adjudicator with a cadre of indoctrinated Sanhedrin to prepare the gallows for the Trump miracle facilitator?

A nation watched intently focused on the scouring of every Russian rabbit hole and coming up empty, and his wife had not pleaded for the Mollusca to wash his hands of the probe. Instead at his side an ignorant sunshine soldier and winter legalist said press on. This Roman imposter would after turning both flanks and coming up empty pin his hope on a frontal gut punch to sanction the cross of triumph. It was hard to believe that a contingent from hell was riding on his success. After all these were not mental or physical giants of the likes the Israelis encountered that caused them to reject God's command to occupy the Promised Land. This lot was the occupying aliens who in power stood for ethic less schools, open borders, sanctuary cities, reproach of white supremacy, a shredding of the moral constitution, annulment of the Second Amendment, billions lost in unbalanced trade, the outsourcing of industry and jobs, and intellectual secrets bartered or stolen by our enemies. To build their voting base they would continue unchecked immigration, millions of abortions, relinquishing sovereignty to a world government and sanction Iran's development of the nuclear bomb by further alienating Israel's existence. Like a page out of Milton's Paradise Lost, these estranged occupiers would insure equality of wealth through a welfare state of mounting debt, high taxation and bankruptcy and turn a blind eye to the slaughter of our police while glorious monuments were dismantled and an allegiance to the flag and national anthem became anathemas of honor. Most likely they would continue the practice of blaming America for the world's problems and the weapon for school killings.

If this is not reason enough to believe that America had lost its soul to the grand equivocation of a matter over mind doxology, then pass the torch and let us die like men. Otherwise, in order to survive we must reverse course and return to the laws, principles and ends that the God of Christianity and Judaism is the only measure of all things. The ruse of socialism, Marxism, atheism, scientism, communism, naturalism and every other whatism must give sway to the positive and negative oneness of a unified monotheism as previously diagramed.

America is under siege on two fronts. First by freedoms tendering elements that few can deny are in a state of flux. Second there is a transparent part of self, called essence whose state of libertine ignorance has become a retro-virus of soullear destruction. On a universal scale, we never fortified the belief why God's focus since the crucifixion was totally westward out of Israel, with America as the terminus for the most fruitful, more blessed and wiser as a work of nationhood. After two centuries, in the language of the devil we have abrogated and denounced that maxim of divine benevolence. When the American soul was once governed as a hemisphere of light is now opaque, foreboding and sinfully encrusted. Before the liberal atheistic entrapment that destroyed our covenant with God, education was grounded in the biblical imperative of the old Satan deluder act.

As an appendage of Israel for too long we've ignored the psalms of David and especially to teach our young Psalm 23. No longer are we captains of our soul as the land writhes in pain of a rotten core. The pillar of words that made us great and full of pride has turned vile destroying civility of thought.

FROM ANOTHER LENSE

Everything presented to wit has not been taught and seldom if ever thought by the Gentile, never most favored by God. Only by necessity, North America, positioned far from the reach of Rome and other blood thirsty autocrats was ideal as a refuge to harvest the two greatest seeds of creation, those of freedom and Christianity.

If this clay miners son of Godly parents was foreordained to discover the power of Absolute One, from which all knowledge flows, what is to be said of hells incestuous command over American education! Even worse is to see the most blessed country on the face of earth in the throes of a despicable Marxist atheistic socialist brigand vying to trade our Christian roots for a despotic tyranny.

When I study the faces of their followers whose psychopathic radical left wing mentality who might well bellow, "crucify Him, crucify Him!". Akin to the diametric extremes of a heaven and hell conjuncture, what is it that bashed this miracle of nationhood to reap the vicissitudes of hells cockroach character.

Anyone who thought the Master Planner was going to sit back and watch His essence of freedom be trashed by these lowlifes, have another thought: Once they annulled prayer and bible reading and pierced the sacred womb was more than reason for reverence to turn into revenge. The lag time for the master spirit before intercepting these demon spoil of the land, began with the 2007 conundrum.

Again, with freedom at stake, as with the Pharaoh of Egypt of old, time and its lag of abuse were rife for God to exert His sovereign might. The election of a young charismatic community organizer on a mission for radical reform was best summarized by his Chicago pastor's remarks! "The chickens have come home to roost in G. D. America." And with the roosters came every collegian transformational fox steeped in the revisionist "Rules for Radicals" handbook. The apostleship of the aspiring protégé of a Daniel Webster like oratory was like "icing on the cake" after a half century united front introit made up of anti-war, God is dead, hate-filled anarchist capitalist detesting move on morons. Unfortunately freedom was not so gratuitous in its passing of the torch to such ebullience that gleamed of utopic optimism. Instead of a bestowed dowry of prosperity a preemptive lag of obscured world shattering economic tsunami welcomed the debut.

After a quick survey of the escalating bad omen it became apparent that a liberal fault line occurred from collateral free home mortgages that burst the bubble sending thousands of home owners into bankruptcy. Federal lending giants named Freddie and Fannie went into delirium sending shock waves throughout the immortal giants of industry causing the nation and the world hemorrhagic rage. As the citizenry gasped few reflect on the constitution structured on limited government with deference to an incentivized will of the people. Had George Washington still been president his first act would have called for three days of prayer and fast to purge the poison and invoke divine guidance. Unfortunately that was no longer in vogue with civil law. Neither did thought register to the Adam Smith model of "Let nature take its course" as when freedom intervened to part the sea and swallow up the enemy, or to march around Jericho seven times as the walls crumbled without a fight. Today's hocus pocus chant relied on the material coelenterate of Marx, Darwin, Freud, Nietzsche, Orwell, Alinsky and other liberal loons.

This age was all about the dogma of scientific reason not about truth. Their slogan was: "its economic stupid" and as the ship of state was sinking the first lady fired the verbal volley stating that "the country and its institutions were in need of a cultural overhaul." Shortly thereafter the pump began priming the Federal Reserve for the greatest financial easing of unbacked greenback in peacetime history. Billions of stimuli would flow into green energy, the rolling wheel industry, cars for clunkers, mortgage relief, welfare, housing, free phones, food stamps, unemployment insurance and a nationalized socialist health care plan without one Republican vote. Even the rhetoric had a socialist transformative ring that castigate the coal industry, the one percent whose owners represent the modern factories and ruling class, the bitter clingers of a societal opposition and an apology tour to the middle east that blamed America for world problems. He would revile the constitution as too negative in restricting an executive monarch by stating he had a pen and a phone which he used as a convenient means to skirt the law. Most memorable in hindsight was his withdrawal of American troops from a stable, yet fledgling Iraq creating a vacuum for the world threatening ISIS caliphate to plaque mankind. He would side with the Egyptian Brotherhood in their overthrow of our longtime friend President Mubarak of Egypt. His kinship with the Brotherhood was short-lived thanks to the Egyptian military. He would take down Gaddafi of Libya who previously befriended America by surrendering his weapons of mass destruction. With his departure Libya became a terrorist haven. After four of our brave diplomats were murdered in Benghazi the administration blamed the incident on a video to allay why requested aid never came to their defense. Every day was like awakening from a nightmare. On one occasion high powered weapons were being issued to drug cartels without surveillance that would kill a patriot border guard and leave a trail of insane attorney general blunder. These were not monarchs of great thoughts and good deeds of honor. One of their slogans probably deduced from the manual "Rules for Radicals" was; "Never let a crisis go to waste". And as a crisis mount that stagnate the G.N.P., unemployment and trade deficit their antidote was to print billions in unbacked paper currency that sent the national debt skyrocketing from nine to twenty trillion. High corporate taxes and stifling regulations were driving thousands of industries and jobs overseas. We can only opine if this was a subtle "scattering" by freedom, as punishment, for its degenerate underling.

Across the spectrum from the highest agencies of government whether of the IRS, FBI or State Department a parasitic mold of liberal antagonism had formed to destroy the opposing party's contender. Just as troubling was when the chief executive remarked of the need for a civilian military, and various agencies began stockpiling reserves of hollow point ammunition.

Although an ill-educated, objectively cultivated populous cared for not, America like Israel remained under heavens surveillance. God's presence in every cell of our being, who lay the frame of our culture, was not about to remand what his inspired founders so honorable preserved. Never discount the role of freedoms inspired Tea Party as the fuse to ward off the tyrants at our inception of birth and were again being summoned to expel the endangered now nestled within. And Adam Smith who God ordained to lay the blueprint for a freedom inspired political and economic system; don't discount the resurrected Moses to unshackle the bonds of these tyrants.

Following is a cursory silhouette of why, by the grace of God, America had lost favor with God. All are an affront to freedom.

- Viewed the constitution as a charter of negative powers
- Skyrocketing debt and deficit
- Industry killing regulation
- Glutting the country with immigrants who hate the Jew and Christian
- Creation of a massive government cyclops-enemy of freedom
- A massive trade imbalance
- Misgivings of a welfare state – when work is the norm
- Stagnant G.D.P. and unemployment
- Insane quantitative easing of unbacked billions
- Open borders with millions of undocumented living in the shadows
- Chain migration – overstay of visas
- Sanctuary cities for lawless to reside from justice
- Insane policy of pulling our troops out of Iraq causing the dread of ISIS
- A madman scheme of giving Iran the nuclear bomb and money to build it and to drive Israel from the face of earth. Did he incur the curse of God?
- Belligerent use of the pen and phone to sidestep the constitution
- Depletion of the world's greatest military force
- Creation of a nationalized health care socialist style system
- Attack on the coal industry and XL pipeline
- Declarative that America is not a Christian nation
- Joining the Paris climate accord as a move toward world government
- Issued high powered weapons to drug cartel without surveillance
- Showed vehemence toward the police by interjecting Justice Dept. into local law enforcement that may have caused a backlash of brutal killing. Denial of surplus military vehicles for states defense.

- Used the IRS to harass conservative groups in order to influence an election
- Used the State Dept. as a front to enhance a family run Ponzi scheme
- Creating a government cabal and fake dossier to destroy a Trump nomination
- Private meeting on a Denver tarmac with candidates husband to discuss grandkids and golf – ya!
- Set up a private server that compromised national security
- After a subpoena was issued thirty thousand e-mails destroyed and devices hammered
- Insane deal of selling 20% of American uranium to Russia while husband received millions
- Failure to aid four brave diplomats in Benghazi terror attack
- Derailing of Hezbollah illegal activities in order to get the Iran nuclear debacle
- Who lied that you could keep your doctor, your plan and lower premiums
- Who conjured the scheme of trans-genderism as public policy
- Who continued the God defying policy of abortion by killing millions of our offspring
- The collusion with Facebook and Google for collaboration on public information
- Last but not least is a shadow government of freedoms endangered who refuse to accept defeat after faced with the "scattering" of 2010, 2014 and 2016

Couple all of the above to an infestation of fourth estate liberal press and better comprehend why freedom has reincarnated Moses to save the land from moronic bondage. Few realize that in order for communism to overtake capitalism they have to destroy both freedom and Christianity. What Lenin never realized was that freedom as the essence of God would never fall prey to tyrannical sleaze. Read the first five books of the Old Testament and witness the miracles the God of freedom performed to pressure his chosen monotheistic nation of Israel. Then ask yourself are not subtle miracles at play in American to scatter the transformational demons as a rapprochement of spiritual accommodation pre-emptive of the American enlightenment.

It would be foolhardily not to mention what can only be described as a miracle of divine intervention. Once we realize that the electron or spirit wave of every atom is Gods DNA programmer of every cell of being, and that his presence resides in each of us the following is with great merit. For this we must return to Eden I where the first man Adam who purposefully had no last name, will undergo a tormented life on earth like no other human would ever see. Cursed by God and banished with his wife and animals past the flaming swords as a disgraced man to wander in shame. Knowing the mercy God accorded the dying thief who was impaled beside him on the cross the following assumption should not be doubted. As the most penitent man who ever lived, I believe Adam who had no genealogical last name, was made to suffer, be pardoned, atoned and redeemed for a mission not unlike Abraham, Isaac, Jacob or Moses. After all if Eden II America was the world's first freedom inspired, Christian enlightened experiment on earth, then should God not insure that its foundation in Godly principle prevail? You be the judge.

While fledgling America was struggling to rid itself from foreign domination a young man by the name of Adam Smith was being elected as professor of logic at Glasgow University, Scotland. His lectures on moral sentiments would lead to his most celebrated work entitled, *"Inquiry into Nature and Causes of the Wealth of Nations."* Its basic theme was that a nation's progress is best secured by freedom of private initiative within the bounds of justice. Both issues surely tormented all of his sleepless nights while on earth.

What made this so extraordinary as to rank among one of Gods justifiable miracles follow the logic. The year is 1776 and the American founders had just signed the Declaration of Independence and were about to debate a new government. By what could only be called an act of fate they will be handed the world's greatest essay on political philosophy and economic theory based on the natural rights of man by Adam Smith. We must blame an atheistic mooring of scientific Marxism that discount that miracle wave that bind in a unique fashion Eden I and its freedom inspired Eden II. Who else in this maddening world would ever propose that human happiness and a nation's wealth was best secured when the individual has complete industrial and commercial liberty, with hands off for government as adopted by our founders. Millions of Americans inspired by his incentivized economic and political system have never been taught the rudiments of why. Or to reminisce whether this the most popular of all names was once condemned, cursed, banished, then like the thief on the cross was atoned, redeemed and resurrected as freedoms emissary in America. Ponder this, before smith would die he ordered that all his manuscripts be burned. Did he envision the fate of America as falling prey to the same liberal assassins that impaled his sovereign Lord?

While we are on the topic of intercessory signs and symbols of divine nature another deserves our attention in the August name of Benjamin Franklin. Although a deist his belief towers above my explanation that God should be worshipped, that the soul is immortal and that it will be treated with justice in another life. Few are aware that when the liberty bell was ordered in 1751 for the new state house, that Franklin had a role in its completion. By his suggestion it would be inscribed with the words; "Proclaim liberty throughout all the lands unto all the inhabitants thereof." This verse was taken from Leviticus XXV: 10. Ask yourself was he acutely aware of America's primary goal as the standard bearer of universal acclaim?

The bell will be rung on July 8, 1776 in its new home at Independence Hall in Philadelphia. When it was being tested in 1752 with a stroke of the clapper it suffered a major crack. It would be recast but again proved defective. Again it was recast and would be moved in 1777 to Allentown to avoid capture by the British and in 1778 returned to Philadelphia. On July 8, 1835 while being rung for the death of either George Washington or Chief Justice Marshal it cracked again. Ironically the crack always appeared below the inscription of Leviticus. Ask yourself if this was an omen of significant prophetic concern?

Thousands of school children huddle around this muted symbol of freedom each year to hear a narrative of its sad history. As I often watched those curious marvels listen attentively and inch closer to touch the bell, I wondered if the story fell short of doing justice to either bell or listener. If the bell could speak would it reveal anything differently about man's greatest quest? Would it say that the crack developed because of brittleness in the metal or was the crack a symbol to the brittleness of a proud people unfaithful to a designated task of freedom?

It would surely state that it was forged with the greatest mathematical precision by the most renown and skilled bell crafters of its day. It would state that not one bell in over four hundred years of casting by the famous Whitechapel Foundry had ever cracked and in fact many were still operable today.

Many would say that this was brittleness of thought on my part for alluding to something unscientific to give speculation to what rightfully did transpire. There is, after all, evidence of possible damage at sea as well as a brutal slam of the clapper on testing which could have caused irreparable damage.

As I stood in the guilt of controversy there occurred an auspicious brittleness in the air surrounding the muted bell. Amidst the hush of the young listeners the silence gave way to a most pleasing and melodious voice. Ironically, it was not the voice of the lovely Park Service narrator, but from within the bell itself. "Please allow me to speak, it said, for I am not only a bell but more importantly I am an extension of a language just as you are. Before the advent of a printing press, radio or television I was a primary means of communication. I was the most natural way to announce all major events such as the time for school, special meetings and worship; Indian attacks, executions and even the toll of death. You might refer to me more appropriately as a messenger and in my case there was something more special than words can explain. When I was being forged I heard the craftsman say in the most tender words that I would be revered and held in endearment above all bells in the whole world. I wasn't sure why but they said that I would sail across a great ocean to be a living symbol in a land bestowed the honor of nurturing freedoms special birth. I did not understand what was so special about freedom but from that moment on I was treated as if I had human qualities. You may say that I was truly human for I was composed of a waist, shoulders, crown, lip and a concern as if I was of the female gender. From my lower rim throughout my waist to my crown I was a series of metal hoops. All were precisely designed and fit to correspond to the composition and density of the metal. Each hoop when sounded apart would produce a different tone and together would amazingly create a perfect chord."

"There was one feature which the workmen said made me unlike any bell ever cast. I was to be a living symbol to extol the dreams and aspirations of all people throughout the world. My message they said would resound to the ends of the earth. They would carve an inscription upon my crown that was to make me the proudest lady in the whole universe. It was said that the message was a suggestion of an elder colonial statesman named Benjamin Franklin. There were no facts to bear this out but the message itself was taken from scripture and the book of Leviticus, Chapter XXV, vs. 10. It reads, "Proclaim liberty throughout all the land unto all the inhabitants thereof." I was now ready for my christening and although there was no ceremony as is often customary, there was gladness over my first sound, which was pleasing and durable. There was a proud feeling for my destiny and I did not know that the nation which would house me was soon to struggle for its own birth. I couldn't wait to sail to my new home."

"The rest of my story is muted and sad. It is a story filled with suspicion and myth and all is lost to the winds of time. There is one thing; however, that we must believe of which freedom is a salient witness. It was not the brittleness of my metal or my hazardous voyage, which caused the indelible crack. It was instead the inscribed task, which would render the strongest metal ever forged to become vulnerable to destruction. It was a mission doomed to fail almost from its inception."

"Before the child America would swear allegiance to freedom the spiritual wedge implanted by the Puritans would be abated by the witchcraft trials. With the advent of independence and a secular charter the substance necessary to build a haven for freedom would rest on quick sand. In effect, my homeland would well up to build a provincial model to freedom that would sedate a world to envy but never the exalted mission that was within its grasp. This would seal forever the incentive to truly proclaim liberty throughout the world. This was an exalted task to emancipate and elevate every species through the power and magic of binary knowledge. Unfortunately, this is a knowledge you were never privileged to hear."

"As a symbol of freedom I could not remain viable while freedom was mocked and the world left garnished in the scars of unfilled dreams. I am not bitter for I understand better than you the nature of unrequited freedom. In another era the spirit of freedom sent one in the flesh with a similar message to be taken to the whole world. It too was crowned and inscribed and then silenced forever as was I. I have but one wish before I leave you. If there should be another opportunity to bring the light of freedom into the world, will you help make it happen? After all, freedom is the key to bringing the richness and fullness of life to every being on this planet. If you can only propagate freedom from your heart through word and deed then gone forever will be the need to defend it on the battlefield with the blood of patriots." With this the voice faded and the air took on a death like stillness. It was obviously time to depart.

As we somberly walked to our buses for the journey home I pondered whether it was proper to fabricate ideas which play upon ones sympathies and emotions. It was then that I realized that I was merely plucking at heartstrings of which the notes lie both on and between the lines of the stanza called life. For certain that is what education is all about. To use the tools and knowledge at hand to lay open the medial lines that stand astride the binary avenues to understanding. Somewhere within the maze of bias, prejudice and ignorance stands the circle of illumination with its trusting light of freedom to extol truth. If that be the case we have defaulted miserably on opening up the multi-dimensional relationship of a complex world which beckons to our young.

One hundred years ago Lenin formulated his United Front or Peoples Front plan for the communists to join any and every organization or disgruntled group to destroy Capitalism. The Marxist model of a utopian socialist world revolution was stymied by what they called the bourgeoisie exploiter class. The United Front was meant to unite against the inequality of wealth for a state ownership socialist planned economy. In hindsight the Russian of old was regarded as someone who knew nothing, cared to know nothing and didn't believe that anything was worth knowing. Fast forward fifty years and like Rip Van Winkle distracted by a material hiatus an unprotected freedom was being infected with a plaque of liberal rot. From education to the courts, press, belief in God, the constitution and highest reaches of government America was awash in an insidious socialist transformation. The evil pathogen was so morphed in the nations DNA that the moment Donald Trump made his heavenly decent down the transitory escalator as if by divine command, the frame of nature gleamed to save freedom from the dread of impious fools.

The voice we heard for the next four years from the left was not to make the way straight by repentance but to attack, investigate, manipulate, interrogate, victimize, wear down, surveil and enucleate, not to serve justice, but to serve the party of death. Never, in American theatre was a duly elected president faced with such a barbarous investigative abomination by a guilt ridden opposition. Their sins of corruption fuel a volcanic adamance to use any tactic possible to destroy this godsend of freedom. To ask what resides at the core of this apoplectic hatred is not unlike the crucifixion that condemned another of God's trusted emissary. In the end their purpose will not be fulfilled for beyond liberal despotism is essential truth and the cruelty of charred word of fact dwarfed by faith.

These fools never thought of freedom as the essence of God whose templet of truth made the Jew his chosen people and America his Eden II inspired evangels. These objective oriented moronic firebrands were in a dying self-destruct struggle to prove the rot of their own existence. Unfortunately that rot was not a people's choice but a decision by an immortal mind of which they lacked control.

In Eden II America, as the universal flame of freedom is reduced to an ember, because its moral soulmate of Christianity has been pulled from its Godly root, the end of reason has arrived. Time remains to reflect on the cave and the revengeful and vindictive wretches who lay the snare. No longer is the good of God's grace our divine fortress except to mirror the vultures now aligned for the kill. Because faith has but one author the battle plans were script centuries ago of which the elements are tempering the will for its introit of tribulation. Only the fool refuses to look at the chessboard and not know that hell is poised to hatch its most poisonous weed.

Because the two most important words of the creation responsible for all creative phenomena are those of positive and negative one whose density is so infinite, they drift into the starter seed word of God. The miracle ellipse that houses the atom I believe is a function of the circumnavigating electron spirit wave. Remember that at the outset there is only light and freedom but no water, air, life giving earth or the new heaven with its array of cosmic furniture.

According to Cambridge University the first mission of hydrogen will be to expand the new heaven into infinity where it will exist opposite the finiteness of earthly hell. Their experiments show that infinity is still expanding by hydrogen atoms. We must also assume that it is responsible for star and sun creation as science confirms of hydrogen being transmute to helium and by nuclear reaction into progressive heavier elements of carbon to oxygen, oxygen to silicon and silicon to iron. It is reported that iron atoms consume energy causing the star to eventually explode. Water will not appear on earth until the eighth offspring oxygen is transmuted to combine with hydrogen in producing the staff of life, water. Prior to water all of the elements for constructing a material universe must be in place. We know the ocean troughs must be carved and underlain with a magnesium base to sustain such buoyancy that involves three-fourths of the total sphere. We can only suspect that the moon is a result of excavated mass. It has been postulate that underlying the mountains is a more pliable aluminum base for accessibility of folding necessary to intercept the rain borne clouds of the trade or westerly flow. Quite a contrast to the belief of some scientists that claim water was transport to earth by asteroids.

Pity the mind that doesn't revel in the miracle of air as the transparent breadth of life. Its major elements of negative numbered gasses will include nitrogen (No. 7), oxygen (8), hydrogen (1) and others of minute familiarity. What is most exciting about air is that of negative charge it will have custody to maintain the dormancy of fire in its inactive state. Negative water will maintain custody of mother earth. How often do we reflect on the miracle that our human bodies are between two-thirds and three-fourths of water composition? That leaves only one-third to one-fourth for the positive charged carbon frame. Just imagine if properly educated on the purpose of the soul what easy access for the negative wave of essence to charge the dynamic custodian of a frail material chaff.

Doesn't it make sense that the main reason for mans bestowed gift of sense was not just for his labor or pleasures of flesh but especially for sight to revel in the never ending miracle in pursuit of the truth that each one conceals. Only by faith of soul can one cross the demarcation line that separates positive charged matter from the pure and eternal of negative essence. Should you care to see what the demon of the dust have done to negate the negative universe where ionizing energies originates open the hood of your automobile. The vehicle and every appliance is inert and useless without the electron. Note what they've done to that primary energy source called "the battery." Readily discernable is a red plastic covering over the plus or positive pole signifying it falsely as the energizing field. As a manner of semantics the poles are reversed making the negative feed as the ground. Electricity always flows toward the attractive ground by using water and air as conduits. When air masses move across earth they pick up positive ions which if warmed are by convection forced to rise. Upon encountering colder high pressure cells of negative charge form fronts causing battlefield conditions that can produce lightening, thunder and stormy weather.

A more genteel miracle is when in childbirth the positive charged embryonic seed of the mother is peacefully encountered by the negative charged male sperm of the father. Isn't it ironic that the only mention of negative force on earth is as the opposite of perfection reflected in an objective grade or deviation from accepted behavior?

As unbelievable as it sounds the annulled absolute word of positive and negative one encompasses a dual encyclopedia of knowledge. One language is purely objective and involves the factual categorizing of the real things of nature. Never is a child exposed to the abridged negative pure that gives all things of matter their DNA qualities of form, structure, personality, and embryonic traits of difference and potential of excellence.

In the quietude of reason sample this select lexicon of the eternal and pure of essence whose genesis is void of objective fire annealed imperfection. All exist for refining the matter molecules of sense to revel in the creative miracle with each passing moment in words like; beauty, love, light, air, water, fire, freedom, life, earth, death, sight, seed, sun, wind, clouds, animals, birds, fish, trees, grass, stars, spirit, mother, father, child, mind, soul, God, truth, justice, honor and every atom created miracle whose truth of cause is reserved for faith in belief only.

Ironically, the most powerful word that stands opposite sense is denied entrance into the august citadels of learning. When Pasteur first discovered alcohol he professed it to be the essence of life. Every miracle of flower is prized for its unique essence of numbered smell and structure. Nothing is more revealing than the essence that gleams from the light-bearing eyes of fiery content that act as a window to express enlightenment for the soul. Then, when the kindred fire that makes for light and sight departs mysteriously into darkness the essence of sight ceases and the eyelids droop for the introduction of sleep. This is but a brief example of how our divine creator transmute by essence a cycle for sense to parse and refresh the never-ending miracle by intervals of hunger and satiety, sleep and awake-ness, inhale and exhale, to purify and atrophy. Unfortunately, the only instruction a child will ever receive on the miracle of essence is from a Friday night urge to partake of the fermented barley or hops that deadens the senses.

The grandeur of miracles evades reason and knowledge of fact as they exalt heavens dominance. Directed at the soul through wordless sound or sign they evade rational understanding as if to jolt the faith of reason. In erudition of truth there is no substitute, even for the improvisational trial and error impostors, dwarfed as a paradox of beloved object. Some miracles that evade the masses are directed at the destined preceptor, while others "like the rainbow, tides, weather, sense, seasons and the like are mere spectacles of God's love.

For the Jew and Christian, miracles were exultations of appeal to steer the corruptible to exalt a path of prescribed righteousness. Every age is charged with the grandeur of miracles – only this one has evaded its reason and knowledge of dominance. Because they appear without factual cause, evading the claim of explanation, science has considered them as mere accidents of nature.

With every waking moment they appear with the first sight of light, breath of air, or taste of water. Feeling the warmth of fire we follow the miracle of sense to satisfy our hunger with the miracle seed born as food for life. We may even catch a glimpse of the species of bird as earth's closest resemblance to a heavenly angel. Seldom do we become conscious of the changing pattern of miracle cloud transporting our staff of life little by little from the ocean troughs. Or ponder of the high altitude Jetstream high above earth that steers our weather, changing pattern every several days. Then there is the sun, stars, and furniture of heaven that grace the animals, trees, flowers, grass and living miracle.

Man needs miracles as surety of being incomplete and imperfect. Miracles assuage our devotion to the things of fleeting matter. Absent the miracles we become mere idol worshippers out of favor with God. Yet, for the Jew and Christian we are the most exalted on earth as recipients of his incommunicable truths of a redemptive life. For Israel it will be by prophesy and direct encounter with God while for America it was by faithful evangel of the prophetic cross. While we mourn for the loss of our young as the age of miracles has turned to madness, they harken to the loss of the greatest treasures on earth. But what should we expect after turning the mystery of truth over to science and knowledge to their liberal godless puppets to journalate and educate solely of matter.

When one party and one political view have self-righteous control as to use it by unscrupulous means these intolerant monarchs have damaged the miracle of freedoms inheritance. It is for this reason that the silent miracles by the son and spirit of freedom are once again making vital a Judea Christian Neo-Renaissance. We witnessed it in the 2010 freedom foot soldiers purging of the people's house, in 2014 the Senate and 2016 the executive. Couple this with the miracle eclipse of 2017 and the election of the swamp draining anti-political Moses and there is a new ray of hope.

As justification for my belief and Plato's simile of souls I believe as live images reveal, the moronic progressives have lost their soul's steersman's wings. And when souls lose their wings they fall from grace abandoned by freedoms inspired trust. The vitality of this free society demands that no one institution of biased thought dominate the whole of society by provoking freedom to intervene.

Some believe, as do many scientists, that miracles are propitious accidents of natural cause. Why, for no other reason would they claim creation had no beginning, that only matter had creative significance, or that the miracle DNA fountain stone of life was implanted in the human gene by aliens. Their belief on what causes light is even more startling, yet they are honored, why? Is it because they predict extending life forever or of the robotic brain ten thousand times smarter which will replace God? Why do they grow in popularity while their moronic vassals destroy life and have already deemed God as insignificant?

Almost daily the ancillary of electron miracle wells our belief in the heroic greatness of our police, warriors of freedom, first responders, medical profession, parents, teachers and coaches and often faithful bystander. It is because they are an underling of freedoms inspired soul and implicit compliment of God. Miracles prevent us from ascribing to ourselves the remedies which come from heaven. It is foolhardy to believe as science prescribes that if it can't be explained by objective fact it doesn't exist.

This crazy thought has removed a never ending creative miracle from a child's education. Many will never hear the quintessential power of the word whose force orbs the soul to the mightiness of miraculous specter, without which destroys the trueness of self-shroud in the inert of objective essenceless rote.

For many students every day is like walking into a foreboding tunnel without the canary to warn them of the sepsis. Never hearing of the mysteries of which no word can explain that tinge of soul is reason enough to know why the torture of abstract senseless fact for an abstract grade kills the spirit. Not one aspect of a matter ontology is designed to make our students good, kind, decent and loving. Never will a child hear the words spirit, soul, God, absolute one or of the most important of all called the miracle of self.

Before we spend billions on putting police in schools or additional million on what is already spent on guidance counselors and psychological staff let's consider the corporate cyclops and those who do while others do in vain to kill the spirit of our young. What ever happened to the heaven on earth our founding visionaries sought and brought with the blessings of freedom? A freedom now bastardized and rendered a paradise of fools. Everything is fraught with ruin on ruin and rot on rot for anything deemed sacred or holy.

Why for solutions do we take the liberal stance that we can buy our way to virtue when the grim death of hell is averse to price? After every tragic killing by our young returning to kill classmates whether Columbine, Sandy Hook or Parkside I ask of God why didn't I have that child considered a bad ass in my class, as seemed to be the rule anyway? Or the other alternative was to give them to Mike Smith, the football coach. Together he and I used knowledge not to entrap but to fascinate and that meant following it beyond the classroom into the real world.

Every year we would take one hundred to Washington for four days where a lawyer friend of Mike's name Richard Hibey, a true patriot, would spend untold hours in the Federal Courthouse explaining the rudiments of government and law. Every day they were lectured by Senators and Congressmen and engrossed in the hearings of both houses. We also took groups to visit the workings of their state government and the entire class to the Gettysburg battlefield. Constantly we had speakers from the outside that comprised a Federal Reserve president, government leaders, spiritual founders and others. One day a week we focused our classes on current events in what was played out as a college bowl contest. All of this required an understanding and creative administration. The corporate school, another liberal spoil of war has outlived its franchise to teach our young. Television, which glamorizes objective fact, has rendered its dual objective counterpart obsolete. Ever since the progressives and their united front have destroyed our Christian roots and its life blood of freedom even the focus on a financial career has proved dismal.

As an appendage of Israel never discount that her miracles were our miracles as well. For her they were directed at sifting a faithful people and a nation to serve as God's earthly kingdom. When that was postponed by divine will, Israel remained the vine and America the branch, for a freedom enlightened Christian inspired temporary reserve for Gethsemanes sorrows. America, like Israel would have its scattering but not of people but of freedoms incentivized industries and inventive miracles. And like Israel's people, Americas scattering of industry and finance are now returning home thanks to a new visionary of a divine trust.

This complete turn of events may be freedoms preparation for a Jubilee year when America is again sanctified in liberty. Few have recall to what that means. Anyone who is familiar with our liberty bell will notice near its ominous crack is an inscription taken from the book of Leviticus 25:10 suggested by Benjamin Franklin for its crafting. Taken from a passage in scripture whereby God is speaking to Moses on Mt. Sinai admonishing the Israelis to honor and observe the Sabbath for the land he is giving them. God's instruction was to count seven Sabbaths of seven times seven which is forty nine and on the fiftieth year, to sanctify the land with a holy jubilee. You ask of what significance is that for America? Count backwards forty nine years eliminating leap year and we approach the approximate year of 1963 – the year reverence for God in prayer and bible reading was banned paving the way for shredding his commandments in the constitution and the market place, a turning point from faith in God to our way of rational allegiance to fact.

After the American Pharaoh pronounced that America was no longer a Christian nation saw the floodgates open for those who had hate for the Christian and Jew. With it came the apology tour, animus for the police and the rise of splinter group united front antagonist to reform the system. In freedoms eyes time had arrived to sanctify our sovereign birthright.

The election of 2017 was more than a natural occurrence of predictable outcome. This one had the super natural qualities akin to the Israeli rerun of Moses leading millions out of Egyptian bondage. Our parting of the red "C" was not of water but of a contaminating 1917 communist ideology as vast and dangerous as all those suffered by the Pharaoh of Egypt. Freedom had run the gambit of watching a liberalized lobomized destruction of everything good and pure that Christian freedom professed.

Praise God for his American Abrahams, Jacobs, Joshua's and Melchizadek evangelicals. All will be sanctified by freedoms patriot foot soldiers of Tea Party fame whose weapon was still the sacred ballot box. Often slandered as deplorable and unredeemable, gun and bible clingers, they truly did what Reverend Wright postulate. They would bring the holy chickens' home to roost in your G.D. America.

These were the modern day sons and daughters of liberty of which the united front band of Pharisee and Sadducee scribe had yet to learn that political correctness was no match for Christian dogma. Neither would they reason that the resurrected Moses was a replica of God's disgust over Noah's son building of his city of God that caused a scattering and confusion of language. The American shemanites had all but completed their sanctuary city pyramid of Lucifer to commemorate a one world order.

When the final outcome of the 2017 miracle sent shock waves throughout the hubs of hell it invoked a delirium tremens not unlike the plaques sent against the Egyptian Pharaoh. The shock of defeat devoured the liberal's heart and darkened soul not unlike the portents of frogs, gnats, boils, locusts and others of physical abuse. Driven from the divine right of the eternal swamp was a momentous shock for the faint hearted lady and her followers of the dismal marsh. More than what beer and hops could quell was the black misgivings of glory and fame of a withering throne. Lacking all humility of the impossible, little did they envision an invincible mind that abhorred the sacrifice of freedom for advent of a craven empire from public lordship by a lowly patrician businessman turned swamp draining specialist, for them he was deserving of the hemlock cocktail.

Never did the losers let known that a united front of red "C" collusion had become a united front plaque that for a half century had infiltrated and destroyed everything good and decent of God's freedom inspired moral covenant. After three years of millions spent scouring every rabbit hole and coming up empty on a collusion charge against the inspiring new Moses all fingers point in one direction and hopefully the cynosure of freedom will not be outwit as to the culprit.

When this miracle worker passed the largest corporate tax cut in history without one loser vote they called it crumbs. Those crumbs have brought more of our scattered industry and finance home to revive a sick economy than words can describe. And when he demanded a wall to keep out drugs, gangs and illegal prey, the irrational lady praetorian in objection suggested, "Cut the grass instead." Did that mean we should give the lawless intruders clean passage through the tall prairie grass so to better avoid any black widows or poisonous snakes? After all, how can you build a good liberal united front voting base without open border and safe passage to their lawless sanctuary cities where drugs and gangs are the modern refuge of true freedom avenger? Don't discount this scheme as another ploy masterminded by the irascible united front, whose collusion charge is but a pinprick on a fifty year Johnny come lately embarrassment.

Let's face it, President Reagan dismantled the old Soviet Union but a bloviated disregard for freedoms vulnerable immunities allowed its communist enemy to poison its blessed seed. President Trump has a mission unlike any president except F.D.R. to eradicate an ideology that has taken America to the brink of disaster. He came as an inspired miracle alongside his trusted Aaron as freedom inspired and although hampered by vain glorious mortal fools due for a retributive justice their cross is his cascade of miracles.

We no longer need 537 house members where one side is all about special interest discretionary spending or freeloader supplementals, unfunded mandates and debt killing entitlements. It's time for review of full retirement benefits after a pittance of time served. And who else has a retirement system which after the working spouse dies the remaining continues the benefit? Also who has a policy that not only pays health and dentistry benefits but vitamins as well? Long overdue is scrutiny due on travel and office expenses and the most troubling of a slush fund to keep perversion charges under the radar. What happened to the time when public service was considered an honor?

FACTS VS. FAITH

A topic never discussed and which has evaded the syllabus and table of contents or a child's study. As this thought must concern a faithful believer, allow me to play devil's advocate and explain why the anomaly. Instead of the label facts vs. faith, suppose we change it to highlight the "axis" of the atom that separates contrasting extremes of a heaven and hell creation. For most of us when we think of the axis of earth we think of its apex as always pointing toward the North Star region of the Ursa Major constellation. Contra wise we think of the southern tip as aligned to the South Pole. But what about the same axis that runs through every human embryonic seed? Its affinity like all flowering seeds is aligned not to the poles but to the spiritual light of life. That leaves the lower or southern tip aligned to the positive ground of earth. One part of our longitudinal alignment is thusly in the material inert genesis of fact and the other upward in the essence of faith. Having left the miracle of which no fact can explain its truth leaves us with a discarded universe whose only explanation comes through faith.

Destroy Christianity and you destroy faith leaving the total human axis to exist on the quicksand of matter. Should we question why in barely two centuries the demon of the dust by undressing a material nomenclature has weaponized an ignorant embryonic mind to war against the faith of its creator God?

As unbelievable as it seems, what began as a beginning in the word of plus and minus one, became a heaven and hell miracle of faith now turned into madness of fact that grows worse by the day. While I yet write a chaotic man made hell may have escaped its demonic vile to threaten human extinction. With God in abeyance and armed with the mightiest of nuclear deterrent why not in a makeshift lab weaponized the most contagious of diseases for a pre-emptive Satanic Armageddon for an ultimate gain of superiority. Never realizing its incurable genie before an antidote is found turns first on its own awaiting a chapter in stealth never imagined. Remember when Rome consigned Christ to oblivion they were resurrecting America to tame an evil world, but it is too late.

Call it an anomaly of reason as we repeat the Roman debacle knowing the miracles of the cross and its Christian blessing have again been impaled by an atheistic science and its deceitful liberal assassins.

Never revealed as truth of fact, no other religion or a people can lay claim the cross and Judea Christianity as reason for greatness. For the abomination never to again be given the honor, as the tribulation approaches, make haste to affirm in which book your name is written.

To look back on the topic of miracles and realize how their fathomless specter has been destroyed by an atheistic science and liberal follower should trouble us all. It can only be explained by a double edge sword of dual addiction. On one side is the cannabis and various hallucinogens and on the other a mind altering liberal enunciated, truth adulterating, God defying stimulant of cascading factual degeneracy.

Webster's unabridged, which I admire for its quasi miracle of objective achievement, merits asking the meaning of "unabridged." Defined simply as being shortened leads me to ask if that means its failure to span the bridge of objective matter with the subjective language of heaven? Is this why the word "faith" is a poisonous non-sequitur of education? Never educated to the truth that fact divorced from faith turned a universe of miracles over to the liberal villains of an illusionary demonic ignorance. The corruption which abounds the nation and the world was not wrought by faith and prayer but by an accumulation of ignorance wrought by inert facts of a liberal tongue, as an enemy of the absolute word of God has made a nation its enemy as well.

Beware the madness of a narrow souled theory and its narrow minded advocate, the free will gift of God's glory was not meant to be bartered away. For just as the miracle of light imbibes then releases darkness, not the reverse, so too as America, the cornerstone of freedom, is not about to fall prey the pernicious disease of a liberal tormentor of tyranny. By freedoms light the hand, eye and its weapon of truth must unify as one to preserve the founders second amendment defense for should we lose, there is no second chance.

In this polarized asylum of dog eat dog mania how does the dual concept fact vs. faith surmount the concept of uniting a world that hates to freedoms essence of love? We've digressed under the stealth of a moronic ignorance that aborted faith in God for matter and money, science and self. No wonder the moral constitution has become a scrap heap of stack-less barnacle. Webster's unabridged defines "facts" as something that actually exists as reality or truth by actual experience. Who among us can find the Achilles heel of that definition? It is' ""that factual reality is truth by actual experience." Not so in this illusionary world where no fact of imperfect matter can prove one causal truth of existence. As for the mundane earthly secular and temporary setting of civil law there are provisional truths that correspond to the needs of the culture.

Just as we've become accustomed to throwing the baby out with the placenta so too because of evil fact we've thrown the faith of God to the liberal bards from hell. God's army of natural law which the founders bound in the immortal constitution was the guardian of Christian faith from the enemy of scientific fact. Fact is all about nomenclature of matter which by natural law is an enemy of faith. By faith the soul of reason can see past the miracle where truth resides in the wellspring of consoling grace and wisdom.

Facts gave rise from the ashes of hells conception whose purpose is amoral. They could build a cross of shame but only faith could turn it into a miracle of glorified and redemptive Christian praise. As pointed out earlier, facts gave birth to a dismal science whose lame experiments of probability do not glorify the creation for fear of slighting the old world monkey.

What a shame and moral crime to allow this liberal brigand to isolate our miracle offspring from the pure universe of perfection, and made to spend every wakeful moment immersed in the charred remnants of a vexatious hell. We must assume that those who call nature God and science as gospel their faith is nurtured by inert non-virtuous facts. Absent the knowledge of absolute one it is difficult to understand God or a beginning. In this winter of despair, does time avail us to rethink cardinal number one as a petition for a freedom inspired second chance? Surely a realignment of our moral will to the 2017 parting of the "C" aka, corrupt collusion of communist influence, may foreshadow a new beginning. If so it must begin with recognition that our secondary universe is an epiphenomena of fused opposites cast from the transmuted word of one as positive and negative force. Nothing of this atom seed creation exists without both in unity of oneness. For construction of the atom building block they become known as the proton embryonic seed and the electron generative essence. Both will become housed in the miracle invincible ellipse bound to either side of a central axis where they acquire the name absolute one.

Because both defy density their origin transpires from the word of God not big bang. From one miracle starter seed one hundred and seven known offspring will be propagate to pollinate individually and cross pollinate to form unending miracle of ubiquitous perfection. Among that perfection will be a junior God of half positive proton and half negative essence aligned to a spinal axis that bisects an elliptical head and body. Attached to the ellipse will be limbs that move fore and aft and as many as thirty one branches of nerve fiber that will ionize every part of the body. They will be interspersed among shock absorbers and cerebrospinal fluid to cushion the delicate brain and sensory system.

To eliminate the soul as the vital principal that charges and protects the inert matter embryo was barbaric. To avoid what every child longs to hear and instead frustrate that miracle with inert fact is a leading cause why in the prime of life, hope turns to hate and if allowed to fester welcomes the drug or even worse the gun. It is not ironic to know that before school prayer was banned it was not vogue for children to have such enmity against their school. If we had our priorities right we would realize the problem is not guns, it is liberalism. To educate and transpire only to the matter and material side of our being is to commit suicide with the miracle of life.

To undress the material word then fabricate and present it for convenient sake of factual worth in pleasure and things chafes the soul of reason. To package the factual nomenclature of the creation and disseminate it as education without its foundational essence was criminal. To educate a child on twelve or sixteen years of such abstract non redeeming mush is what has produced the horrors we blame on the insane, the weapon, and the constitution, racism, sexism, chauvinism, xenophobia, misogynies of an ego-maniacal conservative. There was a time before the distractions of the living room and hand held small screen that replaced the wide screen of endless miracle that by sight alone and instruction from the soil a deep sense of faith gave sanity to the soul. This was accompanied every day in which the word of one was transcending over the school public address system. However, since we've become cloned to inert facts that alone tempt us to be rich, equal, loving and not poor, how has that worked out?

Facts enabled us to split the atom and did that make us safer? When they destroyed God and gave us evolution did they make us more civilized? When facts are disseminated as knowledge who is made wiser, our students or Satan? Does a solely objective syllabus upbraid or degrade ones character? And when prayer and bible reading were banned was ignorance fostered or lessened? By abandoning an ethic and the morality of right and wrong did it make our schools safer? And did the blackboard chart showing humans as evolved from a simian genealogy; did that enhance ones pride or character? Even more troubling was to define freedom as the omission from guilt or blame from standards of moral conduct. And did that not destroy our Christian heritage?

When by the fact of convenience we transitioned from the oxy-pure soil to the market motivators that made Sunday a day of sport did it enhance the character of a people? And when we sublet the large screen of transparent miracle for the small screen and the Hollywood replaced the hemlock with the cannabis sedative, had we become the apothecary of the evil weed. No government law can prevent any of the above and should we rather than focus on the gun, start by banning the scalpel and suction tube whose innocent blood no God can forgive.

Where there is no ethic and no guilt for a liberal insanity gone mad remember that our schools are staffed with guidance counselors, psychologists and one costly cyclops called the intermediate unit that deals with special needs children. It became a political ultra-expensive boondoggle when in the 1950's it was masterminded when the county superintendent was eliminated. Instead of focusing on the NRA, how about the NEA and the AFT who pose a greater threat by their united front liberalism that funnels billions into a party that freedom has assigned as an endangered species.

Imagine what education would be like again with objective facts bond to the faith that allowed freedom to forge the American superpower. We have the man who can turn it around and as well convince an atheistic science to lock arms with creative truth. If this narrative reveals one message it is for the heart of a nation in despair. America, at the creation had a divine mission by an inspired people, not unlike that of Israel. Absolute plus and minus one is the word of God transmute to the living atom seed that will propagate a dual creation.

By now every eye of sense must have a visual of what positive matter entails in relation to the negative of essence. Couple this to freedom as the essence of God and the starter seed of the creation. Because of the negative charged electron God's presence accompanies every atom in its pollinating and cross pollination throughout all existence. Because no eye can ever look upon the light of God his presence in freedom is ever present to command his will through unexplained ubiquitous miracle including that of self. To understand his will of miracle read on his commands to Moses and the plethora of miracles that will lead millions out of bondage on a forty year trek back to their homeland.

Because freedom, his most powerful force in the universe, that made its way from the crucifixion to living seed in America and now defiled is due for deliverance. God has watched and waited for sanity of will through miracle of purification rite in 2010, 2014, 2016, a foreshadowing eclipse, devastating floods, ravishing fires and the liberals obstinance was not broken. Of this I am certain; when the time for deliverance stands between the preservation of freedom and the moronic moral turpitude of a lawless people, on which side eternity stands.

For all to see, not unlike a court room sat the conferees of shame and blame and to the right liberty and truth. For simplicity we could whittle it down to fact vs. faith for convenience sake. By fact, a battle was lost and a rider tossed, but to the chagrin of divine right, liberals and ladies never lose and are never tossed, unless by the protrusion of a collusion. Especially before the final tally was decided from the coffers of the self-aggrandized user, plans were already underway to solicit membership of a united front adversary to lay a trap by false dossier to level criminal charges against her business man rival.

But victory by hook or crook of which she was famous didn't pan out. By hue and cry a special council of blame and shame party lawyers, up to fifteen and all moronic associates began scouring the Russian bushes in search of Kremlin bait. Ironic that after three years of the nation's most expensive witch-hunt nary a clue of collusion is found. What makes this scheme not only sickening to a citizenry of faithful as well as the God of freedom is to ask how such a deceitful evil has made its way into American politics. Clearly the shame and blame of an administration that from its highest reaches said to hell with freedom and justice and wrapped arms around an illegal deceptive spin gathering research of a corrupt party official is beyond reproach. But what should we expect when we murder our innocent offspring at the cradle and preserve our walking hospitals from the grave.

For the losers of pay to play, selling off of US uranium to Russia, secret meeting with Justice Lynch pin and losers husband, use of private server for top secret transactions and cover ups by FBI officials and onerous top brass speaks for itself. Usually in American elections the honest loser picks up his marbles and graciously capitulates, but not this bunch of moronic losers. They turn their marbles into despicable lies laden with their sins and hurl them from a coup de tat shadow government lion's den.

For sure, the world needs facts but without faith they are nothingness. Facts tell us what they supposedly reveal and who or how they dogmatically influence by what they reveal. Custom claims facts to be the foundation of history but what or who is the final arbiter of history? And of the growing mass of inert dust of time do they not reveal more about less in this vast ocean of truth. Of course, they give us simplicity and glamour of luxury, but to fully distract from the wisdom of their essence was an insult to freedom.

In the final amalgam the obscure Muller probe is the frightening reality of a half century death knell when an atheistic science became headmaster of education. Ask yourself, was it the 1957 Russian launching of the Sputnik satellite, or the 1963 ban on school prayer that ushered in abortion on demand that allowed a liberal united front to lay waste the greatest freedom ordained nation on earth.

Faith on the other hand is resolute and unhampered on where it can travel throughout every miracle into its abode of truth. When we reach a point of knowing nothing above the facts we skeptically know, then it is that faith and infinity take over. Likewise when facts make us painful and fearful in our companionship with death – the norm of life, faith is there to give us hope and guide us in the most troubled times.

Without faith of a spiritual ionized soul never can we discover the essence and beauty behind the object of facts. First and foremost facts have no relevance for explaining one causal truth of natural law. Only in civil law do they have legitimacy and even that is speculative as crime is given sanctuary privilege. On earth facts are like bikinis – it is not what they reveal but what they conceal. As we have witnessed those who live by facts suffer an existential self-imposed imperious lawless pride as we witnessed in the e-mail scandal.

Whenever facts use freedom as license they can destroy by evil means such as pay for play, fake dossiers, inter-government conspiracies, use of the pen and phone to circumvent congress in the treaty making power, or to pass a socialist style health care bill. Praise the God of freedom for his intervention to sift from the righteous like the apostle Paul, Adam Smith, our founders, the Tea Party foot soldiers and now the resurrected Moses to undo the curse wrought by giving Israel's greatest threat the bomb and the money to destroy our anointed ally.

For all inanimate objects their vertical axis is propagate from the miracle seed and directed heavenward. The ellipse from which man has acquired his objective mathematics offers both proof of God and why an objective mathematics and its fact is deemed imperfect. Its explanation is explained by the hypothetical number of 360 degrees as the standard for all elliptical or standard circular form. Why 360°? Because it is the only number that is divisible by all digits but number seven – with seven being God's number. Six is the number of the wild beast. By implanting a central axis in the ellipse man is able by using a horizontal mid divider acquire four ninety degree angles. From these numerous triangles are construct around numerous quadrilaterals having four sides and four angles from which to construct a progressive mathematics.

For any factologist of science who needs a sign to foster faith, number seven is that sign and the celestial ellipse its proof. While considering mathematics keep in mind that progressive number began with the digit and cubit. The digit was arrived at by counting fingers or toes from one to nine, the cubit from the elbow to the tip of the middle finger usually 17 to 21 inches. Most interesting about the digit in order for nine to progress further it needed to incorporate the zero of nothingness often regarded as the devils number. Can we surmise that the catalyst that is progressing the world by electron Nano digits, has but one destination into the finite orb of our genesis state of fiery hell? This concept should appeal to the worshipper of their big bang provisional scientific god.

As an addendum to peak ones faith on why seven is God's number – consider this brief and far from complete listing:

- In <u>seven</u> days God created the heaven and earth and rested on the <u>seventh</u>.
- For Noah's ark God's instruction was to take aboard by <u>sevens</u> every clean best and by <u>sevens</u> every flying creature.
- After the ark was readied <u>seven</u> days later the deluge began
- The flood gates of heaven opened on the second month of the 17th day in the <u>seventh</u> month of the <u>seventh</u> day the ark came to rest on Mt. Ararat.
- After Joseph was sold in Egypt he foretold of the Pharaoh dreams of <u>seven</u> good cows, <u>seven</u> good ears of corn and <u>seven</u> bad cows.
- King Solomon will build his house of worship in <u>seven</u> years.
- God admonishes Israel that the righteous would fall <u>seven</u> times.
- Joshua would march around Jericho <u>seven</u> times and the walls crumbled.
- God bled from <u>seven</u> wounds on the cross.
- If a brother sins against you forgive him <u>seventy</u> times <u>seven</u>.
- Reject my commandments and I will chastise you <u>seven</u> times for your sins.
- To the man with leprosy – bathe in the Jordan River <u>seven</u> times.
- <u>Seven</u> letters to <u>seven</u> churches
- The hypothetical ellipse divisible by all digits but <u>seven</u>.
- <u>Seven</u> colors of the rainbow.
- <u>1917</u> Br. General Allen will free Israel from Turkish Muslims.
- 1967 six day war won in <u>seven</u> days.
- 2017 election of Donald J. Trump
- From Revelations: <u>seven</u> spirits – <u>seven</u> golden lamps – <u>seven</u> stars – <u>seven</u> seals – <u>seven</u> congregations – <u>seven</u> plaques – <u>seven</u> mountains – <u>seven</u> lamps – <u>seven</u> kings – <u>seven</u> spirits – <u>seven</u> torrents – <u>seven</u> eyes – <u>seven</u> angels – <u>seven</u> heads – <u>seven</u> bowls – <u>seven</u> trumpets

Eliminate a faith in God and the jubilation of praise for unending miracle and what remains are loathsome ponderings on the nomenclature of things and pleasures of self. The touchpad is its own instant magic factual analogue of continuous quantifying variable to sedate the material matter over mind enthusiasts yet, in truth mind like conscience and soul are not matter and should they be enticed to become so the moronic have overtaken the oxy pure collapsing the empiricism of reason.

In the dual hemispheric mind of positive and negative atom construction what the matter of sense constructs the lobes of reason must inherit. God was masterful in his positioning of his junior likeness between the dual forces of heaven and hell to undergo tempering of the free will. Christianity was America's greatest force for tempering the spirit of reason to the will of God. Through prayer and sinlessness of faith with alignment of the law of God America prospered unlike any other.

It has always been postulate that the traditional conservative law giver carried these principles for safe guard into the highest chambers of national trust. By faith freedom then inspired an inventive spirit that through the knowledge of fact jettisoned a world envied technological revolution. Then after a century and a half the phantom of despair arrived hastening the good of God to vanish in evil deed. The hour of the soul was sent into wordless free flight as freedoms beauty fade turning Washington's dignity into a liberal vulgarity. Like vanishing ghosts our primary industry vanished overseas, leaving empty skulls many to become gambling casinos. Science was extolled as headmaster of education causing prayer and bible reading to exit leaving a liberal objective education to fester the lobes of reason.

With God in exile and conservative belief neutered, the factual fanatics came to the rescue to save the sinking ship. Absent the restraining power of an invincible freedom, the poisonous united front ideology had free reign to inoculate every institution of the culture with an anti-Christian alien social doctrine. Once the antidote of faith succumb an ill-educated partitioned body from soul plebeian had no discernment how the liberal factologist made liberty as the new equalizer of good fortune. Too stupid to realize they were being lied to, the liberal left fascinate on the frailties of mankind to win their new found divinity. Follow the logic. That which makes the liberal left a reality is their ability to turn dis-unity into a way of achieving perfection. By fascinating the masses on the beautiful word "equality" is akin to promising manna to a lifeless soul. Never would they advocate that nothing in nature, the handiwork of God, is equal except in death. Beauty is variety and all things are numbered for a special excellence and virtuous station in life. The beauty of a freedom inspired government is that it is a dispenser of equality under the law.

No one of DNA embryonic code that individually programs each of us in growth, character and potential is so numbered to exist in poverty. For this reason equality of opportunity is the norm and it is the opportunity that is a self-preparedness function. For the liberal left to proselytize a Marxist utopia of a communal equality is a fraudulent claim. Ever since Lyndon Johnson declared a war on poverty billions have been spent on its behalf only to fail miserably in its effect while bankrupting the country. Tolstoy explained it best by stating that; "the more given the less the people will work for themselves, and the less they work the more their poverty will increase." America in just eight years has seen the debt skyrocket from nine to twenty trillion much of which is attributable to a liberal welfare bonanza.

Other areas of dis-unity to garner political hay is the lefts fascination with slavery which as a non-sequitur was a condition that pervaded every segment of mankind over the centuries of man's inhumanity to man. We should thank God that as a condition of freedom no longer is it sanctioned and to use it as a poison pill to arouse hatred is moronic. Because the liberal left has annulled natural law as the universal governance of a dual unity they have assumed sovereignty over the fundamentals of climate control and population, right to life, and its extermination. These two factors alone are the most grievous offenses facing the God of freedom. I mourn as should all of us, of what suffering lies ahead for this iniquitous and shameful grief from inside the sacred womb, and the miracles of His holy word. Finally, what they have done to shred the sacred constitution and its sanctified laws of Moses carved in stone and transplant on the heart of the believer now shattered by the pagan idolaters of an atheistic liberal science.

There is another non sensual principle of cognition as the answer to the conflict of self whose equivocation concerns the essence of the spiritual and fundamental ideal. Being opposite and less intrusive as lifeless matter is the reason of the soul whose tender mercy is the fountainhead of hope, justice, love and forgiveness as the remedy to combat evil. Because its reasoning is super essential and has little bearing on the sensible has detracted from one's ability to seek the measured life. The soul is an immortal miracle that lives within each of us as it assumes custody over a matter embryo transmute to living flesh.

No icon of science can transform the inert proton atom of matter into any living member of sense, yet we forfeit our being to them for our every need. Neither can they conquer death which is reason they should have extolled faith in God to enhance an even greater synergized amalgam of dual being. Should they be reminded that the one who conquered death also gave us the cure for knowing the miracle of life which begins with self?

FREEDOM, THE ESSENCE OF GOD

As humans none of us are far removed from being cave dwellers of a deceptive mind torn between the real and the ideal of fused opposites. We are junior gods on a compass course to surmount the light of truth or perambulate to the darkness of despair. Freedom, light, water, air, fire, the atom and God are all of infinite cause whose dimension escapes objective reason. Had we not fallen prey to the deceitful duplicitous scientific frauds of creative lie and instead was taught the rudiments of a dual creation of diametric extremes the American Eden II experiment could have changed the world. Only by an abiding faith of a divine creator was man the embodiment of dual spheres of heaven and earth with one mission. Unite both in oneness or live in the illusion of both. Never taught the unity of oneness to the most pure, virtuous and moral we must suffer to the torment of the real and amoral.

Make no mistake this nation was not a manifestation of chance but a providential paradise founded at the creation and blessed by the cross. The forces of evil are already aligned to fulfill their death wish to Israel and America. We are the checkmate and with haste let it be known. And if there is a rallying cry it is to expose the predecessor fraud who exacerbate the crisis.

Every day we awaken to a liberal sideshow of baseless inflammatory dirt to impeach a president upon whom God has poured out his spirit. Yet, it is the challenging Neanderthals who are guilty of every sin they've lodged against this innocent emissary of God. Even their voices have become an impediment to the sanity of life.

Further, Mr. President, know that you are dealing with an offshoot of vipers that have made the tree of liberty rotten and its fruit likewise. Your mission is inspired to bring Americans scattered might back home in preparation for your manifest to assist Israel in her last great battle and assure that both our houses stand together and our godly pillars do not fall. When this occurs there will be great revilement but know you have come with the divining rod for freedoms crowning hour.

As Americans, most are trapped between contradictory extremes of universals that pull or temp from opposing sides not knowing which to serve. It's no joke that something is always doing us we know not what. It makes sense that what is up is secure in light and life and what is down is dark and foreboding. Every seed pushes upward towards the light of life, once dead it returns to earth. Nothing living ever seeks death unless the terminal ill. We live in this catch 22 haunted by the paradox of death always questioning if up is eternal and is death a passport to its perfection. Only faith and freedom know the answer. We are transitioned between the plus and minus, positive and negative conflicting universals that in reality are known as death in gravity or alive in spirit essence. Nothing exists without both as the cellular structure of all phenomena. In this regard instead of investigating words from things of matter, truth is that things were made from the word.

Tennyson once wrote that, "if we could understand the flower, roots and all we would know God." I believe this could be revived to say, if we knew positive and negative force we would be God, for both have destroyed every probe of science in search of cosmic truth. Why? Because before positive could become earthy matter whose essence is the downward attractive force and negative the ionizing generative opposing force they both had to originate in the word of one. Unfortunately word has no measurable density yet in its pure form of energy not found on earth it has immeasurable transmutational power. From these two words the proton of matter was transmute by negative pure mathematics. Similar to the way water has changed to wine or hydrogen and oxygen to water. On earth all we know is positive mathematics which is fire annealed imperfect and conceived in a state of protogenic hell. No school ever mentions negative mathematics yet they know we live in a world of opposites. Heaven is of negative retractive charge that minuses into quintessential purity of eternal energy, transmutational power and divine essence. On positive earth an objective mathematics progresses not into infinity but into finiteness of an earthly genesis and amorphous state of chaotic hell. Unless both are bound in unity of oneness a wretched state is replete with an ignorant multitude of lost sheep.

Nowhere on planet earth do we see unity except in nature whose essence of character is made mute and inanimate of expression. Because man was accorded a free will for allowing transmission to the footstool of God also allowed him to challenge God's law of existence. When the governor of a nearby state proclaimed that man's civil law trumped natural law his treacherous honesty spoke volumes of how low and desperate the scoundrel had fallen from truth. Who of the same poisonous sting determined that every ionized battery should have its positive ground labeled with the negative minus sign and the negative inductive pole as the positive plus. This concept alone turned the absolute word inside out by mere corruption of the word of one.

Hidden inside the invincible atom ellipse of plus and minus one is a hidden subjective knowledge for every answer we seek. From this one absolute a universe of miracles is poured out behind which lies truth of which no factual postulate of science dare know. And when it comes to man's claim of control over weather and climate we should opine if this insult to God has any effect on the tempest of a springtime that has a tinge of what preclude a coming age called ice. Let us not forget Shem's Tower to heaven that invoked a scattering or of Cain's city made barren of soil and encrusted in evil.

From the knowledge we failed to teach like the calming comfort of the psalms and the lessons we refused to learn has brought us to a precarious crossroads. Maybe as forbidding as that mortal taste of the forbidden fruit we now find ourselves on that perilous ground that once positioned the cherub with flaming sword as introit to a former scattering.

Most of us spend every wakeful moment enthralled in the visual sense of things never venturing past the axis of one to spend time in the abandoned universe of negative power, energy, intellect and transmutational miracle. In a prior chapter I diagramed absolute one and labeled it as the trinity. Should this narrative fall on ignoble thought at least ponder when the axis is vertical the word of plus and minus one reveals the atom as God's plan of creation. Next rotate the ellipse clockwise 45 degrees and you see the crucified son of God. Continue the rotation another 90° and you envision the pouring out of the Holy Spirit to humankind. God is the sovereign of heaven, Christ the sovereign over earth and the Holy Spirit as the soul's custodian of the earthly body. Contrast this to another trinity of which scripture refers to as the triple six markings of the beast. Fast approaching is its science implanted chip to replace the DNA made permanent by the word of God. Those who refuse the mark of the beast by Revelation will be unable to buy or sell in the market place. No longer does this dreadful thought appear as fiction. America's role since the creation was primed for this coming tribulation. The Jewish people have been returned home as is the beginning of our own scattering of might. Not only are the players of the chessboard providential but so are the rules meticulously plain.

Instead of chastising our adjudicating Moses as our inspired president look east towards Israel and her enemies who are at the peak of power and insolence. While our own nation is in its most vile state of moral turpitude, the dual ellipses of good unified to form God have turned to outrage. All of the blessings she has poured out upon this people must turn from internal chastisement of the inspired prophet and focus on our own united front impending peril. Purge the slanderous insult whose spirit has overcome the sacred ballet box and concentrate not on dismembering the coveted constitution but on renewing the moral infrastructure of our schools, homes, government, infrasonic swamp and media propagandists. Never was the time more crucial to allay the moronic fact for a soul born faith in the God of our fathers. How many who suffer the pangs of children killing children, harken to the multitude of women weeping when Jesus was being led to the torture stake and his reply, "Weep not for me but for your children."

America like Israel will never be conquered from without. Israel has been invaded thrice by invading armies and by famine and her people scattered throughout the world but the land and country by God remained fallow. They would suffer bitterly but by promise of God they have now returned. If this is a sign of the tribulation and second coming, then America as the Jewish umbilicus is rife for a freedom censuring redemption. Don't underestimate the ballot box miracle of 2017 that stunned a nation deeply entrenched in the perversions of freedom, nor don't just pass off as an act of nature the ominous miracle that obscured the sun in the summer of 2017. We must assume this same aberration occurred between the 6th and 9th hour of the crucifixion when darkness overcame the earth, after which the earth quaked causing a rift valley from the Red Sea to the Mediterranean. America is still trembling from three of the worst hurricanes and deadly fires that followed the miraculous eclipse.

Truth is the mother of the seed. If it doesn't spring from the fountain of the soul, striving for higher principles of life, then what remains? In politics, we have seen of truth admonitions of the dead rubbish of partisan deceit. Anyone who takes an oath to defend freedom and in his soul does not know the depths of its divinity is an enemy of its seed. When we think of Democrat as the left hand of God and Republican as his right no better example in 2018 epitomizes which is heaven and which is hell.

Never have the losers of an election become so withered in pride and ravaged of mind, like savage wolves to overturn truth with fictitious lies. A year hence and every false charge of special council stabbed at truth were the sins of their own loathsome heart. When fully revealed, the scar they have left on the tree of liberty should prove a death knell for generations to come.

On planet earth our inferior intellect prevents us through an objective imperfect fire annealed fact, from ever understanding the summation of the absolute. The infinite mathematics of the atom, whose properties of matter and spirit energy defies all human comprehension. Once this divine unity in numbered miracle propagates a ubiquitous variety in seed borne fashion, the matter side of the embryo is timed to ripen to perfection, then undergo the siege of decay and separate for return to its propagative state. Matter returns to dust and the soul its flight home aboard the electron wave. Even the most perfect seed in its struggle to reach the love of light finds itself under siege by the villainous unproductive weed. This Gestalt process of the organized whole escaping all human cognition that involves an orderly process of positive sense and negative essence of natural immunities to ward off attack should concern us all to revisit the nature of the soul.

I would ask earlier if the pillars of earth, air, fire and water knows itself. Because it is from these that the human seed is formed so should we not ask if the seed knows itself. After all, the only thing we know with surety is that "we are," with everything else speculative. We can expound this aphorism to say; we came into this world as part heaven and part hell to face a timely test to matters sense or spirit essence. In the political sense it seems asinine to equate material sense with liberal nonsense and traditional freedom inspired Christian essence with the conservative body politic, but how better to describe the ominous siege we face. Americas founding through to its golden age of the twentieth century saw its God revered and worshipped daily in praise and thanksgiving.

As a young child during the great depression there were no handouts, welfare, free phones, food stamps, public housing, social security or food banks. Many of the financial banks closed never to reopen. Nor was it the government as the almighty benevolence. Instead it was the almighty seed and its germinating good earth that made the signature garden and a saintly mother the god-send of survival. Since World War II this benevolent incentivized industry has come under siege by a liberal caretaker government. To be elected to office had nothing to do with traditional values of freedom or Christianity but by the promise of what they can give for the vote they got. In those blessed days the cellar larder was lined with mason jars of every variety for home prepared succulence. The siege of traditional America began when the Mason jar was replaced by the convenience store once reserved for the condiments the hand could not produce.

We love the convenience but fear the tragedy when it occurs and the store shelves become empty. It is the tragedies that bring our senses back to God. Once we realize that the soothsayers of evolution are dead and gone, leaving no trace of any evolving species, except the endangered on the left and that the God of heaven continues with eternal instruction may be too late. To ask why in the American paradise, the theory of opposites evade classroom utterance and why this forfeiture of the knowledge of eternal truth is likewise buried with the cultural siege of a fake science. The reason why God created light and a transparent medium was not for flight wholly, but to partake of his wonderful miracles. Only two majestic words became the starter transmuted seed of plus and minus one. From the miracle which is no different than changing water to wine or the resurrection from death to life, will propagate to 107 known offspring that will pollinate individually and cross pollinate into this ubiquitous variety of unexplained miracle. By God's freedom inspired America it was our duty to take this message to a pagan world.

In order for freedom to stabilize the seed of humanity it needed a faithful visionary and a secure repository protected from the weed of tyranny. What most plebeians fail to understand is that the seed of freedom unless fused to Christian moral excellence will become a magnet for the most despicable of moronic weed. Two centuries after that bond of goodness was fashioned in the world's greatest earthly paradise that blessed footnote is under vile siege.

Once the Judea Christian ethic died and the root of freedom poisoned, truth and honor depart before the glorious withdrawn light. The light of visionary founders, their glistening monuments and glorious flag whose despairing fondness once blend with the colors of sky now vulnerable to hate. And the wondrous anthem whose fate of a nation rested on its words now dishonored. As with the words one if by land, two if by sea, which that night add to our fate by gallant heroes today lacks the rapture of meaning.

AN ENDANGERED SPECIES

In this fleeting moment of time immersed in the miracle of matter, sense and spirit essence we seek wholeness of being from the dueling antagonists of factual quantity and eternal quality. Neither in tandem crosses the threshold of learning. Education has found a way to end run what is time, dimension, beginning, cause or truth of everything. We skirt the subjective qualifier of what is real and deal with the mundane, surficial and transient. Seldom does the thought of a pure knowledge and mathematics of a pure universe cross the mind. As a result a purely objective syllabus becomes the vitrified menu of an education much like the slag left over as inert in the refining of ore. Slag is also used to define a worthless profession or social group and for this narrative a licentious and endangered profligate of Godly freedom.

Who would believe this great nation nurtured on the divinity of freedom whose restraint of evil shapes all ends, has been basterdized by deplorable slag as inexcusable and damnable.

Regardless of intellect there is a divinity that shapes all ends. If for no other reason trust this divine command to the 95% of the DNA still undiscovered. Such change in people and events are not only a result of age, lifestyle, climate, predatory accident but by corruptible human activity as well. The log or timepiece for such determination I believe rests with the invincible generative electron or spirit nursemaid that escapes all detection. For just as it circumnavigates the proton of every elliptical atom; it also forms a halo around each of us. For this narrative our focus is on the magnificent halo of the white sepulcher where our national stewards are duty bound to exalt a righteous nation in freedoms trust. While glistening pure on the outside, the inside now festers of bitter immoral tongue and jack-ass theory that circumvents the essence of a righteous soul. Many who serve there fail to realize that the freedom they serve is not an invention of man or improvisation of factual probability of truth.

None have taken an oath to uphold natural law over civil law which compromises truth and places self before God and country. These are villains who sacrifice our allegiance to freedoms Judea Christian principles aligned to God's sacred commandments. They've uprooted the providential seed of our founding and poisoned its fruiting stock without a people's vote of confidence. These wretches have made a sham of catering to the discontent, as a means to enhance their powerbase, with a welfare state of bankrupt supplementals, entitlements and discretionary spending. They legislate not by Christian principle and therefore are ignorant of what freedom wills.

As centuries passed and thought turned to knowledge and matter into meaning, so also did cultures and customs cloaked in pagan belief. Over time nature replaced God as the answer to pacify every necessity of mystical concern. A rampant immorality of pagan rite gave God no choice but to intervene.

Where vice prevails and impious officials shrink from honor, God intervenes and justly so in the most glorious 2017 election. Especially when freedom is at stake as we have seen with Saul of Tarsus, Churchill, Lincoln, Isaiah, and now as Adam Smith before him a reincarnated Moses to lead this people out of corrupt bondage. Don't take my word, just study the one sent as being doubly armed and indestructive in his mission. Immediately he instilled new life into a dying nation as a sign of divine providence. His advent was nothing short of a miracle worker with the herculean task left by shameless fools who sucked the nation dry. With both life on earth and death itself a mystery of miracles, when the land becomes morally decimated and eviscerated by fools, and freedoms moral fiber raped, it must intervene.

Never lose focus on our mentor Israel who under cruel bondage saw an abundance of plaques as well as a parting of the sea directed at the assailants. So far America has been spared the plaques unless they are those of the liberal assassins directed at the constitution that incurred the wrath of freedom. Certainly the election of 2017 saw a parting the C^s of corruption and collusion. Let us hope that the liberal villains will soon be swallowed up when they retract under the gravity of truth. If it doesn't happen by natural volition the task remains for the sacred ballot box and the loyal foot soldier honoree adjudged as freedoms faithful.

Freedom is all about unity of difference whereby one side imbibes and consumes the one less virtuous. Examples abound whereby water has custody over land, air over fire, love over hate, health over sickness, light over darkness, freedom over tyranny, good over evil and ad-infinitum for everything from life unto death. Add to this listing that the oxy pure have custody over the moronic illiberal, atheistic science. In our inspired democracy the ballot box is the designated sacred arbiter for a countries purge. Unfortunately, when the Christian ethic and freedoms God were impaled, a moronic liberal lust for power aided by an adversarial Russian united front turned the ballot box into a power broker for the lawless.

The 2017 purge brought to light how ingrained the corruption was and more importantly to oust the endangered species in advance of a cultural revival. Most likely the gargantuan task can only be accomplished by a divine scattering as our mentor had to undergo on three occasions to break an adamant will. If the Pentateuch teaches anything for both the Jew and the insolent gentile is that our God is not only patient but mercifully unyielding. Never fail to discount how he dealt with the Pharaohs innumerous plaques as well as the Israelites refusal to enter the Promised Land and made to wander forty years for what was achievable in forty days.

In my lifetime never have I seen the tendering elements under the stress of biblical proportion. When God pronounced to Abraham that those who curse Israel he will curse should not be taken lightly. When the derelict Obama gave Israel's greatest enemy the Atom bomb and the money in billions to build and deliver it for the Jewish destruction, incurred that wrath of curse on America. For this reason the total element of miracle that propelled President Trump to power was providential. If you want a sign none was more ominous than the eventful solar eclipse that pre-empt the political hiatus along with the worst flooding and scorching fires of recorded events.

To blame all of the life revealing miracles as acts of nature was insane, for out of chaos God created nature. It is not nature that gave us the miracle of sense in order to divine the miracle of nature. Just as we cannot separate freedom from the essence of God, neither can we separate nature from the handiwork of God.

Does today's offspring of those who brutally crucified the Son of God deserve a reprieve for our own crucifixion of his laws enshrined as our trusted covenant? For Israel millions were held bondage in Egypt while in America his blessed word suffered the torment by an atheistic, God hating liberal of factual science.

When the red C of corruption and collusion was driven from office their vile plaques now torment the new Moses. Are not the un-ending probes but heinous plaques at the heart of innocent victims? Is not the blatant slaughter of our innocent of the sacred womb, now approaching 100 million, not a plaque on the human soul? And should we not add the wanton killing of our police to that demonic list? Is this heaven felt wound but an example of the dismal hiss of the demonic enemy whose purge of God is replete with the guile of men? For if not by deceptive cunning why are our schools replete in non-virtuous objective abstract mush of indoctrinated expediency?

God was masterful in creating a world of opposites not only to give balance of oneness, but to make relevant a matter vs. mind dichotomy. There are scoundrels among us so stated Benjamin Franklin upon leaving the constitutional convention. Evidently, he regarded the sacred ballot as fundamental for freedoms success. Give praise to freedoms miracle foot soldier the Tea Party patriot that in three purges would vanquish both houses of Congress, the Presidency and nine hundred and sixty state legislative seats and twelve governorships. If that doesn't portend of a divine over-lordship we are beggarly vain. Lady liberty is not just a three dimensional work of art but an inspired monument of a Judea-Christian ideal of freedom. Until 1952 our immigration laws sanctioned that belief until a culprit lion of the senate reversed its repeal that caused an onslaught of anti-Jew and Christian, unassimilable, low skilled, entitlement prone detractor of traditional values. This would inspire a previous executive scoundrel to pronounce that America is no longer a Christian nation. Belief of many on the left would concur with the insult and its deep felt conviction, that we are a world conglomerate awaiting the mark of the beast and the robotic brain.

I'm sure God in his abundant mercy is aware and for good reason why the crystal ball must become the ballot box to hail God's sifting of President Trump. This modern day Moses was sent to lead this endangered of moronic turpitude out of bondage and liberate the curse of an abomination. In the interim as an act of penitence add this addendum to lady liberties pedestal, "Give me your tired, your poor soliloquy." No longer will we give you free welfare, housing, food stamps, insurance, college tuition, Obama phones, sundry supplementals, trade deficit, crippling debt, budget deficit, depleted military, open borders, thievery of intellectual property, or a united front overthrow of capitalism, Christianity or freedom, the life line of the soul.

UNDERSTANDING LIBERALISM

The road map to understanding anything with certitude on secondary earth is to have clear knowledge of opposites. On earth everything is by trial and error fabrication of fact where as in the retractive pure of essence there is no object only pure energy, intellect, mathematics, law, truth, power and ability to go directly from the concept to the original. Point being: always look to the essence that created the fact before arriving at a decision. Only science is bold enough to claim probability of truth. We on earth are the lower, secondary and substitute always confronted with the contradictory extremes of a dual creation, a dual language, mathematics and contrasting philosophical difference between the liberal materialist and the conservative traditionalist. Even the fool cannot disagree that mankind is under bondage of heaven as the original truth regardless of what the whimpering liberal believes. Keep in mind that their lineage is to materialism, naturalism, determinism, socialism, communism and every ism that is offensive to spiritualism, traditionalism, conservatism and oneism in the beginning word of God.

We have sadly evolved into that corrupting state whereby all events, choices, decisions, and especially education and a dismal science now govern the total knowledge and word of Gods natural laws of truth.

The apologetics of truth have been made hostage the visual communicators of a liberal invader of the electron nursemaid of God. Surely God foresaw the day when the miracle eye as window of the soul would distort his truth and abandon the language he died for on the cross. These substitute demons have banished all that the brutal suffering spoke of in love, justice, forgiveness and faith to overcome the plaque of evil and its horror of sin.

In politics many confuse liberalism with liberty and the rite of free expression in human behavior, equal rights, and civil liberties. Devoid of natural law standard those rights have been expanded to mean freedom of choice in standard of life, marriage, transgender accommodation, open borders, sanctuary cities, civil disregard for traditional monuments, the flag, its anthem, and the police. In the halls of Congress and its former executive branch they have shown adamancy towards our mentor Israel, and end run the Senate in granting Iran the terror state enemy of Israel the atom bomb and money to finance the evil intent. They would construct an evil snare by fake dossier to destroy an election rival, clamor for open borders, sanction amnesty for millions of undocumented, blame America for the world's problems and man for global warming. Their myopic view of duality has pit fact against faith never mindful of the "Omnia exevent mysterium" meaning, all things pass into mystery.

After destroying the commoners' mind of reason with the belief that man and science are the measure of all things, the nature of God was not about deference to the mediocre and moronic. The lesson the demon failed to learn was that the stone the libertine builders rejected – would become the cornerstone of the culture. Anyone of sane mind should have been educated to the miraculous handprint in the human gene as that rejected cornerstone. This, the greatest sculpture of human providence whose supreme elegance direct the embryonic growth and unique character of every being was the adamant stone and Holy Grail cup rejuvenator of life, that has been sought after since the crucifixion.

Once the pure knowledge of an eternal God was made siege by the liberal soothsayer never would the children of light understand how embryonic growth was bond to a rejuvinative life. For just as no two seeds, two snowflakes or two people are equal by design; embryonic growth goes beyond development of the objective frame. It transcends the mental as well to insure safe passage as an adored attribute of the God who lives within. How else in an oxy-moron setting was this child of God able to walk the tight rope of opposites and align his free will to the pure of knowledge, freedom, and divine essence hampered by an objective gravity of sense. Never discount the enigmatic halo of electron invigorance that circumnavigates our being like an angel guardian that steers the wind, air, water and fire, or the freedom that governs all form and motion. As I look back over the frailties and follies I am convinced that to be of oneness in God is to be inspired, shield and served as every other miracle.

So Virginia and the millions of snowflakes living with the fear of tragedy stop asking why and with two simple words; "I believe" follow your destiny. The Holy Grail cup, that Christ and his apostles drank from at the last supper, as the symbol for the rejuvenated life is not lost as historians believe. It lives within each of us and awaits the mere asking to companion your life. Just imagine if this were not a universe of contrasting opposites there would be no surety of judgement for anything. Call it a miracle but diametric extremes begin with a dimensionless heaven in bond with an opposing dimensionless hell from which we have a dual language, mathematics, intellect and propagative composite seed. Enter now the free will of choice absent the imperial past of forced will and know that both freedom and will exist to champion the consciousness of truth.

Whether traditionalism or liberalism will win over self depends on the most superb mystery of life as to which will conquer the incarnate of carnal self. This makes all of life a savage pilgrimage of dueling contenders. In America, as with idol worshipping Rome before us, the forces of hedonist liberalism and pagan determinism have reached the zenith of war with the mystical lore of heavens absolute. Without the spiritual muskets to save herself required the divine sculpture to again intervene. Alive on the national screen these modern day marauders of liberal tongue had become mosquito critics with an envenomous sting.

No longer was the patriots dream to make a heaven on earth but of an unconditional subversion to make hell the jeweled crown of earth. Although no modern school includes in their curriculum the topic of a dual creation has dealt a serious flaw to the knowledge of truth. To make a case for the merits of liberalism, our most logical starting point, is with the dual strands one positive and one negative of the ineffable handprint of the DNA. Depending on a child's foundational motivations to the things of matter or to a mooring in faith most likely will serve as the compass course for ones destiny of belief. Often time's tragic events illuminate what only the soul understands. One thing for sure without the Judea-Christian enlightenment as the safeguard of freedom, America would never have arisen to become the world's envy.

When the Christian evangels veered west from the cross into Europe on their way to America a divinity followed their every step. As a wonder of the world the greatest industrial age based on a freedom inspired individualism was nothing short of an inspired miracle. To this day without this outpouring of divine benevolence the east would still be feudal in standard. We can only blame the stealth of that greatness on ignorant liberal policies of power and equality which by nature is a non-sequitur. The hidden nexus of this divine benevolence of a technological inspired bonanza by individual expression was made manifest by the indwelling spirit of God. Ask yourself as proof, even in this age of wonder could anyone develop from scratch a typewriter, radio, telephone, rubber, strike oil or develop a pencil without the assist from a watchtower assistant angel of transmutational power.

I had an opportunity to meet a believing dirt farmer commoner who lived with his mother during the poorest of times in a rolling hills area of the Appalachian plateau. His verifiable claim was that on three occasions during his sleep, his deceased father and Jesus appeared to him with the request "to dig." They would return for an answer and a third occasion to tell him where to dig. All he knew was that as a young boy playing near a stream that ran by his house he noticed bubbles of air on the water. Taking a tin can and puncturing a hole in the top and placing it over the bubble, which he thought was sewer gas, then striking a match it exert a large "bang".

With no money and with orders to dig by the apple tree he knew it had to be for oil. His trek began by asking locals to invest in buying a rig to drill for oil. He would acquire enough money to purchase an old wooden rig and set it up by the assigned apple tree. Well below the depth of where the hammering bit was designed to go the gusher was so great it blew the rig out of the ground catching an oil fire, which could be seen from 35 miles away, in my home town. This would be the largest oil well east of the Mississippi River.

As an instant millionaire and a story filled with intrigue, when I met up with him he was not only broke but all of his expensive accouterments were impounded by the IRS and no regrets because the travail allowed for him to take care of a family member's medical problem. This antidote tale of faith speaks volumes unlike what any liberal would comprehend. In this kaleidoscope of miracles I firmly believe that most of what was prophesied to Israel is still being manifest in unbelievable fashion in America. Freedom as the essence of God through the Holy Spirit is in these crucial times pouring out his spirit in dreams, visions and portents in the heavens.

Most of what I write has come to me in sleep while the matter molecules retire for needed rest or, by tributary of known and unknown source. Anyone who fits the mold of the emblematic donkey as an obstinate ass of uncircumcised purity, they have been snookered by the liberal obamination cabal out to destroy what freedom sanctioned. This is my belief, that the oppression with which the liberal cabal has leveled against freedoms liberating deliverer has become a retro-viral plaque against the provocateurs. This because of the curse acquired from the Iran nuclear deal. This is a harsh reminder to the liberal Big Bang era activists that live by the trial and error of matters thorns, who use demonic tactics to castigate what freedom wills. What freedom is unveiling through its faithful emissary is the manifestations of a pitiful and melancholic disease of liberal sense. To castigate the honest conservative victors as bible totin', gun clinging, deplorable, un-redeemable wife humiliator had crossed the moral threshold of judgmental authority.

Freedom knew in advance that Christianity was being pulled from its root and reason for revelation of the DNA as the world's greatest sculpture of any century. That leaves us with a dying exultation of hail to the liberals dissident chief who echoed from the dust the phrase; "why not the Norwegian!" Had his soulless avengers realized that freedoms newly installed prophet was only relaying the land crying out for repeal of the dreaded Immigration Act of 1965. A memory few have recall when a majority of our Christian lineage was turned away for entrance of a majority that had hatred for the Jew and Christian. Not for their basic theme of equality but to enhance the liberal voting base.

Liberalism, as an advocate of equality was a concept dilatory and demeaning to natural law. By creation nothing is equal except death as the norm and opportunity to excel. Instead of equality whereby there is universal sameness the opposite is true with every seed different and variety the cause for beauty and excellence. A recent Russian discovery claims that not even two snowflakes are identical.

Equality is a nebulous term that has allowed the liberal mind to use as a hammer and sickle to brow beat capitalism into a false utopia of equal ownership of the factors of profit, production and distribution of goods and services. This is contrary to a freedom inspired individual incentivized American wonder of the world.

Liberalism is an advocate that fosters individual freedom in unrestricted human behavior, equal rights, civil liberties and principles of politics. In America it has become a seductive weed to choke the traditional constitutional belief in a divine absolute. By focusing on the civil laws of man and nature as his God has encapsulated a neo-paganistic belief in things of nature and the icon of science for the dealings of life.

Is this not a sampling of antiquity when worship ranged from the snake as an amulet to a man serpent, moon goddess, or a jade god who hatched all of nature from a world egg? Does this not sound like the breeding ground for a liberal minded evolutionist. After all, their prophet Darwin could just as easily been studying snakes as iguanas. Does not paganism beget atheism, socialism, Marxism, Freudism, communism and liberalism as rogue gallery enemies of freedom inspired Judea-Christian belief?

To believe that we are immune from the following fanaticism think again. We have our own "Big Bang" Prometheus who created man from clay and hatched nature from an evolutionary world egg. Our deity of creation evolved from the brine as the most fit by natures unique method of selection. That is quite similar to Nun as the ancient god of the ocean, Keb of earth, Mat of truth, Nut of heaven or of Tristo, Woden, Thor and Frigg which later became our present day Tuesday, Wednesday, Thursday and Friday. And does not our belief that man is the animal most fit correspond to the animal deities such as the calf, ram, goat, bull, snake, sow elephant or the scallop as the symbol for passionate sexual love. Today that symbol is the oyster and Viagra goddess of sex. Not to be denied is our beloved icon of science whose homage is not unlike the deity Mat – goddess of truth or of Apollo who symbolized fertility, death and its terminus. For the unbeliever they still believe their icon will extend life indefinite. Instead, what they have accomplished is how to destroy life in the miracle womb and then extend the old into walking hospitals.

What is most clandestine yet visually a companion of all of us at home and around the world is Osiris, represented by the lotus flower. What makes it sacred is its five petals which to the alchemists and hermetic occult believers represented the four limbs and head or the five senses and five digits of the fingers and toes. More specific it corresponds to the four points of the compass and the zenith. If we put this into practical terms we see its powerful influence in the precisioned minds who built the great pyramids, sacred cathedrals and towering obelisk such as the Washington Monument or the one in Vatican square.

Before I reference the largest and wealthiest fraternal organization in the world and among the most charitable whom God will inspire to bridge the natural and supernatural with lineage to Osiris and its ancient codes. Their belief that building is what creates not only majestic structures but better people, better communities, better societies and a better world. Now pause, as a clandestine quasi supporter of Osiris the pagan god and reach inside your wallet and take note of the dollar bill. On the front is a picture of Washington and on the back the seal of the United States. Take notice to the pyramid and at its apex the eye of Lucifer. Directly below are the Latin words: "Novus ordo seclorum" whose translation means "New world order."

What should concern us is not that forty-four of the fifty-six signers of the Declaration of Independence were free Masons whose quest for the Holy Grail saw it hidden in the medieval building codes of the Masons whose buried secrets were often placed beneath their Cathedrals such as Notre Dame or the Temple Mount in Jerusalem. For this narrative we should be mindful that it was not nature that sifted these quasi-shamanistic believers to enlighten the world through geometry as the gateway to reason, but to accept God's calling to establish a temple to freedom as the means to pure knowledge through Christian faith. Our present day imperative is not to vilify our brilliant founders for what they believed or deportment of lifestyle in what they owned but the blessings that made America the greatest nation on the face of earth. What should concern us all is to debunk forever a former chief executive setting the stage for a one world order, under the shamanistic claim of global warming, climate change or world distribution of wealth for starters.

In the same urgent conceit we must come to our senses that a scientific materialism overlaps with an atheistic world view and esotericism to counteract the Christian espousing hierarchy by pursuing a materialistic, mechanistic and atheistic world view that would come to fruition by means of a Marxist, communist contemporary consumerism. Never discount a contemporary untied front of which the term collusion is but a longstanding ploy to destroy. Our new president must be applauded for repeal of the Johnson Act and his renewed pledge to Israel as firm indicators that the problems facing America span the trinity of economic, political and religious siege.

Never in the history of America has a duly elected president faced such vile and caustic rejection by an opposing party and its derisive press. Since the 2016 ordained vote of no confidence, they've exhibited themselves as a spectacle of damned fools. From their towering oracles of stone and steel languid in spirit and barren of the divine profusion of faith, they trumpet the endangered voice of liberal dross. In times past when the nation slumbered in war, bread lines, dust bowls, or Tammany corruption, freedom of the press always tendered the obstacles through goodness of grace and tempered mercy.

Not so for a ruthless epoch of entrenched corruption that neutered freedom, annulled God, Christianity and the spiritual soul. Today's endangered liberal species no longer is guided by God's natural laws and purifying commandments, believing they alone know truth of what is morality. Maybe they should remove the blindfolds that reveal in this creation the only truth is of a total miracle and no man dare claim it. Even the icon of science with its fire annealed fact is forbidden its right of discovery.

Civil law or man's law can be hazardous as it allows the liberal anti-god crusader to turn freedom as the essence of God into anything goes to preserve a moronic liberal bias. Pure freedom is a restraining force of evil that is opposed to open borders, sanctuary cities, transgenderism, fake news and dossiers to destroy a political candidate or to harass religious groups to influence an election. Civil law does not stir the divinity within us, nor revel in heavens eternity amidst civil discord. The first sign that a proud nation is in demise is when a freedom inspired press trumpets the voice and dross of a corrupt party that turns honest defeat into scurrilous rebuke.

Never taught is what has caused such vitriol and its contagion that plaques freedoms reverent love and holy light. Few are alive today to remember being warned of the paltry united front. This topic should have dominated the free press and the national education association for the last hundred years. Nary a word for Lenin's communist ploy to destroy by peaceful means, the American freedom inspired individual incentivized capitalist system. The plan called for socialist sympathizers to infiltrate every union, government agency, political party, news agency, education professorship and disgruntled group to mastermind American demise. Pure freedom, as the essence of God and natural law require constant vigilance and the sacrifice of patriots. Don't tell that to the demons who have forfeited that trust to regard freedom an invention of man and anything goes by civil law.

Who remembers the Red Scare of 1919 when a series of Bolshevik mail bombs led to a round-up of 5000 suspected communists being arrested and 249 deported? Fast forward to World War II when Russia will become our ally to defeat the Nazi tyranny and how afterwards she will mastermind a series of unfinished wars that will begin in Korea, then Vietnam and finally the Middle East. At home the genie will escape its evil vial as the nation erupts in war weary campus riots.

By 1952 concern began to mount that communist inroads were made in the highest reaches of government, labor unions, education, the press, university professorships and college campuses. Finally in 1952 sub-committee hearings began of suspected 205 communist subversives who had infiltrated the State Dept. Having been drafted for the Korean conflict and in basic military police training at Fort Dix I was assigned as chauffeur for the company commander that allowed me to watch the famous McCarthy hearings on television. For these the first ever publicized national hearings it did not bode well for the young Republican Senator. Although a public was divided on the outcome, evidence would accuse him of overreach by badgering witnesses, attacking President Eisenhower and producing no evidence of subversion. Personally, I find correlation to the present day corruption trials of the State Dept., FBI, and Clinton and Muller probes. Regardless of who the defendant, most of the accusations revolve around irate slurs between the Democratic black caucus and the Republican panel members. This allowed someone like Lois Lerner of the IRS to take the 5th Amendment, go scot-free into the sunset with full retirement. The bait and switch collusion special hearing of Robert Muller should go down as the greatest witch hunt in American history. Why is the poison pen refusing to come clean on the most corrupt political party administration in pay for play, fake dossier, and collusion between justice and FBI, selling of U. S. uranium to Russia, etc. while focusing all attention on helping the Democrats destroy freedoms anointed miracle ministering Moses.

The year 1952 will also shock the nation as the atomic secrets are passed to the Soviets by the Rosenberg spies. Both husband and wife will be executed. Anyone alive in 1957 will recall the trepidation of waking up to learn the Soviets had placed the first ever satellite into space. This earth shattering event will propel science as head master of education paving the way for school prayer and bible reading to be banned in 1963. Ten years later the Supreme Court will repeal abortion laws in 46 states. By 1964 we were full-fledged in the Vietnam War. Bloody riots will break out at Kent State University which will dovetail with President Johnson's Great Society war on poverty and the infamous Voting Rights Act of 1965. Theodore White will claim this act will do more to change the culture of America than anything else and who can disagree.

I was a teacher in 1963 when a liberal atheist in a nearby school district sued to have school prayer banned. After appeal by a liberal court an American tradition would exit education and steamroll across the country eradicating every moral restraint of Christian tradition. The vacuum created in our schools was quickly replaced with drugs, sex, rock and roll bizarre deportment and courses hastily revised to upbraid self-esteem. Then came Columbine, Sandy Hook, the Amish School and today Parkland. An ignorant populous and its representatives with a secret taxpayer slush fund to hide their own perversions, never cared to connect the dots.

As the united front was in its hay day with war in Vietnam and protests raging at home for civil rights and counter culture demands the congress placed a finger in the dike and lowered the voting age from 21 to 18.

By 1945 the Soviet domination of Eastern and Central Europe led Churchill to announce that the "Iron curtain of Russia had cut Europe in half." From 1947 well into the 60's America will follow a vigilant containment policy against Russian expansion. Labor leaders had to swear they were not members of the communist party. In 1959 when I entered teaching I also had to take an oath that I was not now nor ever had been a member of the communist party.

One more revelation to contribute to the summation when I entered teaching every member had the freedom of option to join in any fashion the local, state and national teachers associations. Most joined the local and state ignoring the national whose influence in local concerns was dismal. That was until by surprise in the early 60's our local president returned to advise that before adjournment of a national conference the motion was made and passed making it mandatory for unification of membership, thereby killing the freedom of choice. What this did was fill the coffers of the Democratic Party with one of the nation's largest contributing unions and loyalist membership. In conclusion, as a silent coup d'état is in play. God has intervened not to save a chosen people but to reclaim his inspired Christian nation from enslavement. Since World War II America is under a reverse plaque such as his chosen people suffered while enslaved in Egyptian idolatry.

Today, in God's mind it is a liberal idolatry that has enslaved his essence of a Christian enlightened freedom inspired Eden II promise to the world. The many liberal plaques that wounded God and crushed his truth to earth were eclipsed by fire to rise again. That miraculous summer eclipse, the same as occurred between the sixth and ninth hour as Christ hung on the cross, was I believe, a sign that the fear of God had sent his sword of fire, faith and power to his inspired Moses. For the doubters opine on this surety of triumphant trinity of installing a godly gate keeper to the Supreme Court, his rescinding of the ecumenical dreaded Johnson Act, and the mending of the American umbilicus with our sacred appendage Israel.

Contrast the plaques of the God inspired Pharaoh with the plaques this man of steel has inherited from the serpentine demon of the dust liberal. A neutered God, corrupted freedom, vilified Judea Christianity, biased press, and coup d'état to destroy the triumphant Moses. Continued vilification by the deep state abuse between justice, FBI, and media, destruction of God's unborn, war on police, open borders, nuclearized enemies of freedom, depleted military, illegal immigration, shredding of coveted commandments of God, and bankrupt welfare state.

LET'S MAKE AMERICA BLESSED AGAIN

Chances are few can disagree with my assessment of why America has become Hells-Demi-Paradise. Many will however be taunt or festered by a compilation of knowledge never disseminated because it was the spiritual nectar of the soul. For this I stand firm behind the provocateur as the liberal neo-pagan neo-barbarian, demon-crat and rhino republican.

Because few are alive to remember when the God of creation was a major part of our other self and was responsible for an Americana destiny of greatness, the will is gone to reverse course. There does however still exist enough of the faithful and a quasi-sacred ballot box to satisfy the peril we face.

The challenge we face dwarfs the revolution, civil war, great depression, two world wars and natural disasters. Why? Because freedom as the essence of God and its soul mate of Christianity were our blessed guardians until both were ungracefully defrocked by a demonic purge. In its wake a socialist brigand of outlaw demon-crat have germinate to choke what remains of a miraculous tradition.

Because they huckster on the theme of equality and free everything an ignoramus gentile neo-pagan doesn't see it as a giant swindlers Ponzi scheme. Free health care and college loans will bankrupt the treasury. When this happens as it did in Russia in 1917, they turn on the land owner and capitalists to nationalize the land, then expropriate all production and distribution of goods, confiscate your weapons and begin a mass exodus into slave labor camps or gulags. Think it can't happen here? You have an ole Bolshevik socialist gaining steam among the ill-informed gargoyle that hates the country and should be given a one-way ticket back to the hell hole they came from. He loved Russia enough to get married there so bon-voyage you crafty Marxist.

Anyone who thinks equality is possible won't find it anywhere in the God ordained creation. Why? Because the infinite mind believed that variety not equality is the blueprint for beauty and excellence. So beware when the socialist huckster preaches equality when what they mean is that once the power hungry despots have your approval they will then dismantle every capitalist institution and make the people the newly enfranchised owners of all goods and services. A great ploy for the ill-educated gullible that only have to look at Venezuela, Cuba, Russia, China, Iran or N. Kora for the truth.

Time is running out for the faithful of Tea Party fame to unite and oust the demon-crat socialist and render his party to the ash heap of history. God is preparing the way for a truly conservative Supreme Court and district courts to repeal the 1963 Supreme Court ban on school prayer and bible reading and the 1973 Roe vs. Wade repeal of abortion laws in 46 states. We must put an end to allowing illegal non-citizens the right to driver's licenses which gives them the right to vote. Beware of changes in the voting rights act by the House democrats as they have nothing else to run on except to create sanctuary cities and states where ex-felons can hide out who also have voting privileges.

Finally, since I began another multi billionaire has entered the race to buy off the divine material right to be president. We can now add another volley to the demon-crap anti-American rhetoric that casts scorn at the nation's beloved farmer. Only a moron could vulgarize this sacred occupational genesis of human life. Will someone remind him that when this earthly handmaiden of the soil is replaced by a biased technology the cities will die and America's return to its original calling. Amen!

Let us begin on this exulting task whose threadbare theory of freedoms life is directly relying on one unerring individual, namely you. Nothing will satisfy the soul more than for freedom to know that once again God is sub served as the moral adjudicator of the American culture society waits to obey your cherished wish to announce an individual greatness fully armed, chaste and spiritually committed. Then listen for the splendid whispers from freedoms death to again bestow its blessings that is if we form unity of sense to essence wisdom will overcome the odds.

SIN-OPSIS

Much of American conscience is undergoing a cultural delirium tremens psychological withdraw of disbelief. Like the deadly Corona virus whose genie has escaped its vial without a known cure only to be accompanied by its vial antecedent anti-Christ enemy of freedom. The former is a harbinger of death the latter a despotic tyranny whose false promise of free everything will lead to the expropriation of all means of production, distribution and wealth of human toil.

I have saved for last why the word God which lives in every electron atom generated cell of our being is a concept that none greater is conceived. The diffused liberal mind is most revealing of God when they exhibit a disdain for walls, borders, boundaries and even axial lines of demarcation as separate heaven from earth, fire form air, water from land, faith from fact, good from evil, love from hate, man from woman and all opposites from life unto death.

I like to think of the left hand of God as the positive attractive gravity of earth and the right hand as the negative and electron generative essence of all material form. Once this duality is breathed to form the building block atom a neutron invincible wall must keep separate these two absolutes. Once they become "real" in the human cell where they communicate with one another they are under custody of the soul which by electron ionization, purity of health is maintained. The electron transverse wave whose origin is in the aether high energy fields of heaven is the primary generative source for all cosmic form and function including life. Its source of human vitality comes not from the ingestion of food but the conscious thankful praise of faith in its provider.

Never do I look upon a seed and not praise the miracle. The same should occur when one marvels of pure freedom as the essence of God.

Because every cell is a seed of God we by the atom seed of conscience should with every breadth praise God, as sovereign over creation, His son, the sovereign of earth, and the Holy Spirit made manifest when on the cross He redeemed our sins. For the Catholic faithful they should include the Mother of Christ and His messenger apostles.

Stereoscopic vision and the sense of touch allow us to discern that all of nature exudes in this silent duality. Unless we envision this wall of division between the corruptible of object and the essence of pure subjective essence we labor in vain.

Never did I imagine a time when the demon-crat liberal government oriented despot of slavery would become obsessed with removing the border between God and Satan, legal immigrants and law abiding citizen, male and female, good and evil, natural law and civil law, the victim and the accused, the proton and electron, the atheist and the Judea-Christian, etc. Unless we revise our education system to restructure it on the foundational principles of absolute plus and minus one and the duality of opposites aligned to the moral laws of our constitution then the church age is over and demise by tribulation is at hand.

This the most important election of our time highlights that we are in a cultural revolution wrought by the 1917 Marxist tyranny. God has intervened by sending us the swamp drainer but are we up to the task of moral reform to take God's freedom into a destitute world for another thousand year reprieve? For certain it won't if we allow a liberal ruse to out flank Godly freedom.

"Off the record" what if this pandemic is a sinister ploy by an adversary to drive President Trump from office and reverse his adamance? Be sure to vote!

ABOUT THE AUTHOR

Jack Hall is a former teacher of American history, Freedom Foundation George Washington Teacher of the Year award winner and Outstanding Teacher of Secondary Education recipient. His previous books: *God's Literal Plan of Creation vs. the Great Satan Generation of Viper, The Spiritron Sperm and Education, Tea Party – Patriot or Villain, The Scourge of Liberalism and the Universal Lie, Miracles and Madness.* All are a roadmap to save the country, its constitution and freedom inspired conservative beliefs. Books can be purchased on Amazon or Barnes and Noble.

www.ingramcontent.com/pod-product-compliance
Lightning Source LLC
Chambersburg PA
CBHW031133250726
48655CB00002B/649